# Early Pr‹

"*Unmasked*, quite literally, challenges the way we see ourselves. It is an honest look in an unfogged mirror. Taking us through a process of deep reflection, the self we see in the mirror by the end of this uplifting and empowering book is nothing short of a self worth knowing and a self worth loving, fiercely.

—Puja Kanth Alfred, Counseling Psychologist, EFT Master Trainer
(EFT International), India

"There are breakthroughs within these pages. *Unmasked* gives you years' worth of therapy in a concise, easy-to-read manual that will shine a spotlight on an easily overlooked truth: you deserve to be your own priority. Through deep understanding, shadow work, and the application of a transformational tool, EFT, Catherine Duca shows you the way to an otherwise elusive "better self" and "better life." If you are too busy, too preoccupied, or too financially burdened to commit to long form talk therapy, this is the book to read."

—Michael Markey
Educator and award-winning sports coach

"So many books out there talk and talk about how to change one's life, but don't provide the tools required to do it. In *Unmasked*, Catherine Duca takes us, step-by-step, through the murky maze of our human vulnerabilities and flaws – the very ones we bury under emotional disguises – and places us on a clearer path to authenticity and self-acceptance. Now I can say to someone who is struggling in life, go read this excellent book to find your true, inner self."

—Dr. Concetta A. Butera, Chiropractor, MS in Nutrition
Traditional Usui Reiki Master, Metabolic Balance Coach

"*Unmasked* takes the reader on a journey with simplicity and compassion, showing the way to access understanding and self-acceptance. Then, it provides a tool for healing. By the last pages, you may hear yourself saying, "I am what I am and THAT is okay!"

—Loretta A. Imbrogno, RN, DC

"In *Unmasked*, Catherine Duca hands us a permission slip to come face-to-face with our fears, delve into our personal limitations and come out the other side. As a former police chief, lawyer, and corporate, crisis manager, I've seen people struggle with the manifestations of inner despair, imposter syndrome, and an overall feeling of hopelessness. This is a handbook to hope and emotional freedom. A must read in this mindboggling world."

—Lynn Centonze, JD

"*Unmasked* is deeply touching as well as educational! You will not only walk away from this book with a newfound empathy for yourself and others, you will gain an understanding of an effective stress-release tool, EFT, that you can put to use immediately."

—Angela Furnari, LCSW

"*Unmasked* could not be timelier. At a point in our history when many of us are feeling disconnected, Catherine Duca draws upon her own life experiences and work with clients to offer us a potent training program to achieve emotional resilience. She not only provides insight into our self-defeating behaviors and patterns but provides specific tools to navigate our way out of them. An impactful and inspiring book, *Unmasked* helps us connect in ways that will love, lift, and empower us."

—Jeannie Park, LMSW

"*Unmasked* is not just a self-help book or a manual to a happier, fulfilling life. It is a journey; learn the many faces we hide behind and the road that led us to *feel like we had to*. Catherine Duca demonstrates techniques to shed psychological masks and facades and become your true you. It's a Hero's journey and if you feel like you're hiding, read it. When you get to the last sentence, you'll feel a tremendous sense of accomplishment. I did."

—Kyle Torjussen, Media Sales

# UNMASKED

## Discover the Hidden Power of Your True Self

Catherine A. Duca

EMOTIONAL FREEDOM PRESS

*Upper Montclair, New Jersey*

Emotional Freedom Press
Upper Montclair, NJ 07043
www.CatherineDuca.com

Cover and interior design: Mayfly Design

ISBN 978-1-7360375-0-8 soft cover
ISBN 978-1-7360375-1-5 ebook

Publisher's Cataloging-In-Publication Data
(Prepared by The Donohue Group, Inc.)

Names: Duca, Catherine A., author.
Title: Unmasked : discover the hidden power of your true self / Catherine
    A. Duca.
Description: Upper Montclair, New Jersey : Emotional Freedom Press, [2021]
    | Includes bibliographical references and index.
Identifiers: ISBN 9781736037508 (softcover) | ISBN 9781736037515 (ebook)
Subjects: LCSH: Self-realization. | Self-confidence. | Social
    desirability. | Authenticity (Philosophy) | Alienation (Social
    psychology) | Interpersonal relations.
Classification: LCC BF637.S4 D83 2021 (print) | LCC BF637.S4 (ebook) | DDC
    158.1—dc23

Printed in the United States of America

✲

*To my dad, who sparked the kind of conversations
around the dinner table*

*that made my career, this book, and my
mental health issues possible.*

*If you're looking for me, I'll be outside, playing.*

# Contents

*Note to the Reader* ............................... ix

*Introduction* ...................................... xiii

**1** | **You Can't Love Anyone Until You Respect Yourself** ........................ 1

**2** | **Deconstructing Shame** ...................... 9

**3** | **The Authenticity Gap** ...................... 15

**4** | **Another Year** ................................ 35

**5** | **Who Needs Enemies When We've Got Ourselves?** ..................... 43

**6** | **Let There Be Dark** .......................... 57

**7** | **Families** ..................................... 63

**8** Walls, Shields, and Cover-ups .................. 71

**9** Psychological Masks and the Faces
of Our False Self ................................. 101

**10** The Bridge ..................................... 137

**11** What is Tapping and What Can it
Do for You ..................................... 143

**12** Use The Technique of Tapping to Unmask
Your Limitations and Access Your True Self ... 157

**13** Tapping Vignettes and Dialogue for Masks ... 169

**14** Getting Unstuck: A New Identity ............. 201

*Suggested Reading and Resources* ............. 223

*Acknowledgments* ............................ 225

*About the Author* ............................ 228

# Note to the Reader

While there is never a good time to doubt ourselves, to doubt what it is that we think or feel, or to lack the confidence in our right to be happy, deserving, and worthy individuals, doubting now is especially perilous.

I am in the business of talking to people about what keeps them up at night, what it is that unnerves, hurts, frightens, and paralyzes them. This is an intimate arena, to say the least, and as a psychotherapist, being given access to it is a privilege that is not lost on me, not for a moment. The turbulence of these times is causing more and more people to not only contend with sleepless nights but to seek help for them. One patient said recently of her bedtime restlessness, "I used to not sleep because I felt the ground shifting. Now I can't sleep because it feels as though it is crumbling beneath me." Undeniably, many are grappling, as is she, with a sense that their psychological, emotional, and spiritual foundation has a fault line.

I have found it impossible to listen to my patients' personal conflicts and struggles without hearing the unease, however vague and unnamed, that has arisen from the life-changing health, economic, and social calamities that have befallen us at the start of this decade, the effects of which are far-reaching and incalculable. Whatever lies ahead, functioning as an authentic, independent thinker is perhaps more crucial than ever before. Why? Because if we were ever mistaken enough to fantasize that someone was coming to rescue us, those imaginings have all but faded. If, as children call out to their parents to come into the dark room to chase the monster from under the bed, we had any illusion that someone, anyone—a leader perhaps—was on the way, my brothers and sisters, no one is coming. We are home alone.

Now more than at any other time, it is up to each of us to shoulder the weight of where we are headed, as individuals and as a collective. We can no longer expect or wait for others to do for us what we cannot do for ourselves. Each of us is responsible for our own consciousness and, given these times, is being called upon to help lift the consciousness of one another. To bring a sense of peace to our planet is to first find it within ourselves. Avoidant, passive, superficial, histrionic, self-absorbed, detached, foggy minds will do little to bring comfort or clarity to anyone.

Key to this book is the belief that we each play a profoundly important role in the lifting up or the tearing down of our self-worth. The former can only be achieved by the clarity of our own thinking while the latter comes as a result of escaping it, of masking those aspects of life, or ourselves, that seem too painful, too unattractive, or too frightening to confront. Our enduring habit of looking away from our darker impulses, thoughts, and feelings, hiding them behind "can-do," cheerful, "all's well" personas places us at risk for going through life more suppressed than free, more false than authentic. To be oblivious, out of touch, or detached from the deepest part of who we are is to live life with a certain impoverishment, overly dependent on more knowing "others" to tell us what to do to be happy. We must be able to trust ourselves, trust our judgment, and trust our competence if we are to have the courage to look under the bed ourselves. To avoid taking this adult stance is to chance becoming overwhelmed by much of life. When this happens, we are more likely to numb the discomfort with all manner of meaningless distractions and anesthetizing tactics.

What follows in these pages then, is an exploration that looks at how we as individuals may become better contributors to the world by becoming better expressions of who we are. In the strictest sense, when we transform ourselves by becoming our truest selves—true beyond self-censorship, true beyond self-limitation, and true beyond self-delusion— we become empowered human beings. And when we do, we invite others to do the same. This is true whether our partner is someone with whom we are intimate or a nation of people of which we are an intimate part.

Amid the unpredictability of this moment in time, there is a growing awareness that we can only give to others what we are capable of giving to ourselves, that having the clarity to see others as they are requires us to see ourselves as we are. Just as we human beings cannot know completeness without embracing the good, the bad, and most especially the ugly that we have disowned, neither can a society hope to realize its wholeness until its members respect themselves and one another. For when we do, when we finally do, we will have found courage in the one and only place it can truly come from: our own self-worth.

It is an honor to take this journey with you.

# Introduction

It's an easy mistake to make. And many of us make it.

The truth is, we cannot beat ourselves up into becoming a better person, shame ourselves into becoming a stronger person, or chameleonize ourselves into becoming a worthy person. Those who go through life convinced that these are the means to that precious prize called love will likely become disappointed, disillusioned, sick, depressed, anxious, or perpetually stuck in life. I speak from experience.

I offer this book as an accessible reference for whenever a person feels stuck in life, or doesn't know themselves well, doesn't know what it is that they really want, or even what their basic rights are in relationships. My clients have often asked, "Is there a book I can read about that?"

Now I can say, "Try this one. It's based on more than twenty years of the experiences of others who have struggled with these same soul-draining dilemmas and have not only found a path forward but have traveled it authentically." If you have been criticizing yourself into a more satisfying life at the expense of who you truly are, you too can find an authentic way forward in these pages.

I have long been interested in the twin problems many of us carry deep within ourselves: a critical voice in our head (which causes us to beat ourselves up) and the lengths we go to in order to hide the deeply held belief that we are not good enough the way we are (which leads to the creation of personality masks and cover-ups); our feeling that, unadorned with social trimmings, looks, degrees, status, possessions, or pedigree, we lack some basic qualifier that entitles us to take up space on this planet. These two factors taken together express and drive a fundamental belief in our own inadequacy.

The ideas in this book deal with how we feel about ourselves and take a personal look at the conversations we have in our heads in which we are hard on ourselves and all too often harsh, judgmental, biting, and even cruel. Some of the questions contained herein will serve as a speaker for privately held thoughts, amplifying them so that we may unambiguously hear the way we speak to ourselves on a near-constant basis. With the volume turned up, it is much harder to escape this inner dialogue, which is reflected in the outer dramas of our lives.

How we feel about ourselves affects virtually every aspect of our lives, from the way we function in friendships, in love, and at work, to how we navigate the ordinary and extraordinary changes in daily living. Who and what we think we are informs key choices and decisions we make and live by—the ones that shape the trajectory of our lives. Of importance to me, and I trust to you, is the level of awareness with which we approach these all-important decisions. Are we guided by our own emotional compass, for example, fulfilling our life's purpose and potentialities, or do we take a more passive, compliant stance and live according to the needs and expectations of others? Do we live by our own imaginative vision or do we exist to fulfill the vision of others? At the end of the day, do we live according to our own principles or do we chase the approval of others? Do we bury our real self beneath a facade or psychological mask that has us feeling like an imposter, or do we speak and act from our innermost feelings and convictions?

Of course, this book does not provide the answers to these questions. I doubt any book can. What it does instead is ask you to *live* within these questions, to grapple with their layers and implications, to find your own identity beneath the one that may have been imposed upon you by well-meaning others in your life or by the necessity of circumstances. The guidance provided is grounded in the belief that how we relate to ourselves has a direct bearing on how we relate to others, and that being able to discern the visible from the invisible programming that runs us from childhood not only matters, but matters a lot.

I hope to stimulate a deeper understanding of how you and I got to be the individuals we are, to examine which of our behaviors either support or subvert our self-respect, and develop a deeper understanding of what it means to live a more authentic life. When you and I are courageous enough to be our true selves, to think independently, we honor the reality of our past and are more likely to honor this in others. By accepting and integrating the often-contradictory facets of our personality instead of allowing them to spar with one another, we function as a more-unified whole, our values are more aligned with our intentions, and our intentions are aligned with our actions. This is what drives an empowered life.

# CHAPTER 1

# You Can't Love Anyone Until You Respect Yourself

You've heard it said a thousand times. "You can't love anyone until you love yourself." Though a familiar, gauzy cliché, what does this really mean? Is this worthwhile advice? And is it even true? Well, yes, it is true and here's why: of all the relationships we have, the most important, it turns out, is the one we have with ourselves.

You and I sit in the midst of a vast and almost limitless network of relationships—to other people, circumstances, and events—but it is the relationship we have with ourselves, the one in our head, that is the most enduring and hardest to escape. If we are not on "friendly terms" with ourselves, as one of my clients, a twelve-year-old gymnast once told me, "Nothing really great can happen. We're the common denominator in everything."

Boy is she right. There isn't a single aspect of our lives—from our level of self-esteem to how we see the world, to the ambitions we strive for, to whom we partner with, put up with, or pass up—that is separate from our own self-evaluation, an internal and deeply intimate sense of what it means to be the unique human being each of us is.

Indistinguishable from this personal view of how we see ourselves is a parallel one: how we are seen by others. The need to be accepted by the larger world and the people in it, especially those whose love and respect we most desire, is of extraordinary importance. For many, this can feel equal to and even greater than our own self-acceptance. When what the world thinks of us carries more weight than what we think of ourselves, we are tempted to base our identity less on our intellectual and emotional good judgment and more on the opinions of others. The degree to which we do so and allow these opinions to eclipse our own, ignoring the factors that made us who we are, is the degree to which we ignore our personal reality and the facts of our lives. Like fake "chicken soup" for the soul, we feed ourselves a diet of false, hand-me-down interpretations of who we are and where our true value lies.

Thus we can develop a type of personal detachment, a sense that we are not in touch with ourselves, that we don't know exactly what we think or feel or quite what motivates us to behave as we do. Given the obvious consequences of living relatively disconnected from the "why" of our actions, it makes sense to ask ourselves some important questions: What is behind this all-important need to be accepted, and how do we gauge when we have attained enough of it? Exactly whose approval or acceptance are we striving for, anyway? At what point will we even know if we have received it? Most importantly, what if what it takes to be accepted by others is at odds with our own deeply held values? Does it even matter how we look in our own eyes, or is our self-approval swallowed up by a greater need to feel loved?

No one wants to be alone, after all.

One of the main factors that separates humans from other animals is our ability to think, reason, and develop a consciousness, a higher awareness and understanding of our own needs, behaviors, attitudes, and emotions. Our consciousness asks questions like these, and our consciousness will either explore or run from the answers. Whichever we choose—the deeper dive of inner exploration or the nearest escape hatch—these questions and the feelings they stir do not disappear.

What do I mean by "the relationship we have with ourselves"?

I am referring to our internal dialogue, the mental exchange that occurs between the "I" who is aware and the "me" who does stuff (takes action). These conversations, whether we realize it or not, affect our capacity to live according to our adult desires and competencies.

Why can't I just be happy?

When will I finally have what I want?

What am I missing?

What is my purpose anyway?

Do I really matter after all?

Most of us do not wear these questions on our sleeve. In fact, we go to great lengths to cover them up, to look as though we are the sort of someone to whom such questions never even occur, since we are likely to interpret them as signs of weakness. But ask we do in our most private and deeply personal search for answers. We ask these questions of ourselves, then listen very closely for the answers.

You might think the inner voice that responds, the one we trust, would just whisper the wisdom we are waiting for. You might expect it to point us in the direction of positivity, meaning, or happiness for that matter, and gently nudge us toward our best self. We would gladly accept the advice to lead a better, more purposeful existence, wouldn't we? But instead, the voice in our head comes in braying, practically hee-hawing its certitude and uses it to kick us smack in the middle of our mind and, as luck would have it, often right in the middle of the night. This harsh mental critic, a supposed authority, has only one answer for our earnest questions. The answer is cut, dry, not very pretty, and according to the strength of its conviction, airtight: We are simply "not good enough."

## Self-Alienation

I have observed clients for whom no matter what problem(s) they come in with—anxiety, depression, addiction, intimacy, loneliness, self-sabotage, heartbreak—their problems are symptomatic of a deeper, hidden cause that can be traced, almost without fail, to a common root: they don't feel as though they are good enough the way they are, that unless they possess characteristics associated with desirability, they doubt their innate value. Beneath their polished exteriors, like so many, they feel a gnawing sense of "less than." Wearing this identity label much the way one wears a name tag at a networking event, they are fearful that others may "read" their secret label and discover the shame they carry for feeling inadequate.

## Hello. My name is . . .

"Something's Missing."
"I'm an Imposter."

"I'm Not an Adult."

"I Can't Get Close."

"I'm Hiding."

"If You Get Close, I'll Run Away."

"I Need You So I Can Feel Whole."

"I Don't Want to Grow Up."

"I Want to Be Taken Care Of."

"I Don't Want Anyone to Need Me."

"I Need You to Need Me."

"I'm Really Angry."

"I Hate myself."

"I Feel Empty."

"I'm Afraid to Have Dreams."

"I Refuse to Get Excited."

This deep-seated fear of being found out has given way to a basic human reaction to develop a protective armor, a camouflage of sorts, meant to conceal our inferior qualities while emphasizing our shinier, more acceptable ones. This camouflage is remarkably interesting and largely made up of the traits that are directly opposite of the ones we try to cover up.

Here is a simple example of how it works: Say for instance, something happened in your early life that made you feel stupid. And say there were consequences for this that felt dire at the time. Maybe someone laughed at you or mocked you. Or maybe you were singled out and ridiculed. Or maybe you were told that you were stupid, and no one wants to be friends with such a person. The experience was scalding and left a permanent impression. You felt awful to the core, the shame almost unbearable. To soothe the emotional burn, what might you have done? You may have said to yourself,

"I will never give anyone a reason to call me dumb or stupid ever again. I will make sure of it!"

You may have vowed to never be in such a vulnerable position in the future, and to make certain of that, you became a "smart" person. Even if you were intelligent by nature, you may have placed a heightened emphasis on "having to be that" in order to shield yourself from potentially humiliating criticism and judgment. By compensating for any perceived lack in this area and to protect yourself from future attacks, you crafted a disguise made up of the exact opposite trait for which you felt criticized. Offsetting the pain of looking stupid and hiding the humiliation that you felt, you devoted yourself to always appearing intelligent, no matter what.

Shame you felt back then is something you may still carry with you. Your unconscious hope is that your "smart" person exterior will ensure that you never look stupid again. Your determination to avoid feeling intellectually inferior and to prove that you are *not that way* likely became your unconscious mission. You may have adopted a mask of "know it all" to conceal your perceived deficit.

Yet the important thing to remember here is that the shame from the original event does not just go away. That shame lays dormant just beneath the surface of your persona. If it so happens that you find yourself stumbling into a vulnerability puddle brought on by having your "stupid" nerve triggered, you risk either a meltdown or a defensive blowup of titanic proportions because you haven't addressed the buried shame. The shame exists as an active component of your psyche that is always on a low simmer and easily boils over when just the right nerve is touched.

These opposite traits are then combined in a way of being that keeps us locked into a specific personality role: our *persona*. These roles and their accompanying masks are what many of us rely on to ensure acceptability and avoid rejection. Deliberately though unconsciously crafted at a young age and perfected over time, their effectiveness is two-fold and paradoxical: on the one hand, these tightly worn masks keep us safe from criticism and judgment. They are compensations for deeper, more uncomfortable feelings and exist to hide our shame and keep us safe. On the other, a great deal of our psychic battery is used to monitor and maintain the tight seal around our masks to avoid further vulnerability leaks. The effort that goes into keeping the seal as tight as possible siphons our vitality for other things in life. Without realizing it, we can feel fatigued, bored, flat, or deadened inside because our unconscious attention is preoccupied with making sure our vulnerability is kept under control. Most of us are completely unaware that this is what we do to feel safe and accepted and have no idea of the high price we pay for keeping this going. We are unaware that the price is self-alienation.

Self-alienation happens when:

- We want to be true to ourselves, but somewhere deep down we feel we cannot allow ourselves to be.
- We want to worry less about what others think of us, but in the back of our minds we do not let our guard down.
- We want to be close to others, but we do not risk being vulnerable.

To help ourselves deal with these fears, we develop a false self, or as it is also known, an idealized self. This polished exterior that we show to the world is the result of censoring the parts of our personal story that carry the most shame, those pieces of our history that we believe would surely get us laughed at, pitied, or ostracized if they were exposed. One of the most striking features of shame is that it creates an underground bunker of sorts deep in our psyche and then jumps in, becoming insulated by layers of self-deception and denial. It stores memories of humiliating things we have done or that someone close to us has done, the regretful or remorseful acts we have committed or witnessed or the exploits or bad decisions that were thrust upon us. These shameful experiences, more than anything else, determine how worthwhile a person we feel we are. Or aren't.

# CHAPTER 2

# Deconstructing Shame

If you are one of the few people on the planet who has never felt it, shame is that cringey rush of self-ridicule that coats your insides from the thoughts down. It always involves other people, the real ones standing right in front of you (you're always expecting them to show up with their piercing gaze when you're about to stick your neck out, like give a speech, deliver a big presentation, or offer up a dissenting opinion about something) and the ones you've internalized that appear as the critical voice in your head (you're always expecting them to show up with their piercing gaze when you're about to stick your neck out like go on a first date, a job interview, write a book), for without judgment there can be no shame. Shame asks, "What will they think of me?" Its mantra is, "If they knew who I was, really knew, they would walk away."

In the very instant that shame takes over, you can feel as though your entire existence is being discredited. "Shame attacks" steal all logic and overrule evidence that you were a good and decent person just minutes before. Shame suffers amnesia that you have an organ donor card, for instance, that you insisted on nursing your mother-in-law through weeks of hip surgery at your home, and that you gave the small spider in your basement a stay of execution by coaxing it for twenty minutes into the piece of crumpled tissue you pulled from your pocket. You had a private moment when it felt better to usher it to the garden, alive, rather than see it swirl to its watery death down the toilet. Ah, shame, the one-stop shop for self-loathing. With its short memory for successes and its infinite one for imperfections, shame lays the groundwork for the shadowy veil of secrecy and scrutiny that awaits.

Shame goes beyond guilt, which is the thought that we have done something bad, that our *conduct* is unbecoming a living organism, to the all-consuming conceptualization that *we* are bad. *We* are unbecoming a living organism. Shame is the in-our-bones belief that we are inferior, broken, mis-wired, less than. With this said, who in their right mind would volunteer to warm up to shame? Answer: almost no one. Who should? Almost everyone. Why? Because the less we look at our shame, the more we cling to the masks that hide it and, in the process, hold our authenticity hostage.

There is a connection between the amount of resistance (fear, discomfort) we have in facing the most tender, truthful, vulnerable core of our being, and how rigidly we adhere to our masks. By not facing our deepest selves, we remain at a loss for how to handle the deepest truths of our past. This insufficient awareness of our shame leaves us incapable of moving beyond it. Ignoring it or pretending it doesn't exist does nothing to dissolve it and instead serves to reinforce it. Our shame wall only becomes more fortified. The stronger the shame, the stronger the cover-up. We can walk around projecting an image of assurance and self-confidence on the outside and yet secretly shudder with a sense of deficiency on the inside.

We are resigned therefore to walking around like divided, masked, inflexible beings with a huge shame secret. No wonder we are stuck. We are stuck behind our shame wall.

## Exposure

If you were to ask 100 people what they want most in life, the vast majority would likely say "happiness." Press them further, however, and you might be surprised to learn that many are willing to do whatever it takes to get there . . . as long as happiness doesn't ask them to gamble with the mother of all risks: emotional exposure.

We spend considerable energy dodging relatively minor mishaps, such as looking silly, messing up, or putting a proverbial foot where it doesn't belong. On a deeper level, managing the anxiety associated with appearing unintelligent, needy, weak, insecure, lonely or, heaven forbid, vulnerable, requires more effort still and are reasons enough to play it safe. And if playing it safe also happens to mean playing small, well that's just the price of rejection-proofing our lives. Making sure that our insides don't leak through to the outside is the guiding principle for the vulnerability-averse among us.

Cue the wall. I've learned from the many smart, capable individuals with whom I've had the privilege of working that this invisible wall is reflected not in the conscious or lofty recognition that their inner landscape has a fault line, but more in the puzzling and nagging logjams that show up in one or more major life areas: relationships, finances, physical and mental health, work life, and creativity, among others. Logjams that can be detected in stubborn patterns, in the promises they've made to themselves but have seldom kept

(I've got to lose this weight!), or as goals they've defined but stopped short of achieving (I'm going to clean up my clutter this weekend. I mean it this time!). I've seen it show up as the happiness they've desperately wished for but have rarely experienced (When is it going to be my turn?). These problems feel shameful and intractable, around which a great deal of psychic pressure has built up—pressure from the frustration, failure, and future stakes of staying stuck.

If shame could speak, it would sound something like, "If you really knew . . .

"How lonely I feel . . ."
"How enraged I feel . . ."
"How lost I feel . . ."
"How insignificant I feel . . ."
"How jealous I feel . . ."
"How empty I feel . . ."
"How unwanted I feel . . ."
"How forgotten I feel . . ."
"How unattractive I feel . . ."
"How undeserving I feel . . ."
"I wouldn't be worth loving. No one could possibly love a person like that."

This is the stuff cover-ups are made of. This is the stuff about which we would rather die inside than expose. This is exactly the place in our heads where we've decided it's a good idea to hitch our self-worth to whatever has a better chance of being accepted: everything from our outward appearance to our achievements, from our savvy business ideas to our social media profile, from taking care of others to putting our needs last. This is where, without realizing it, we have surrendered our spirit to shame and have been withering inside a little at a time. This is where we instinctively knew we had to split ourselves in two if we wanted to belong. What resulted was an internal gap as we learned to deny our hurts, disappointments, and confusion and carry on as if things were going according to plan. At some point in time, we stepped into that illusion and began to call it home.

Overcoming shame requires a new emotional zip code. How do we get there? The surprising answer: follow the gap.

\ \ | / /
## CHAPTER 3
/ / | \ \

# The Authenticity Gap

When there is a persistent difference between what we want in life and what we have, the disparity that results is our *authenticity gap*. When we believe one thing about ourselves but portray an entirely different image to the world, when we make promises to ourselves which we seldom keep, we owe it to ourselves, no matter how uncomfortable, to actively explore this incongruity and try to understand its meaning. A commonly held tendency is to think that such a gap is fleeting, accidental, or merely the result of external circumstances and will fade with time. In truth, this type of looking away will only compound the problem.

What do I mean by taking an active rather than passive approach toward freeing ourselves from gap living? Individuals who have an active orientation to their inner life enjoy taking responsibility for their own questioning. They don't depend on someone else to figure things out for them, nor do they expect others to compensate for their shortcomings. In fact, they delight in taking curiosity-driven ownership for the quality of their own lives. If they notice that their way of behaving does not line up with their deepest values, they don't lull themselves into unconsciousness by shooing away such realizations. They investigate the factors that drive it. If they are plagued by a gnawing discontent, instead of sweeping it under the rugs of rationalization and distraction, they root out the cause.

Those who assume an active role in their own emotional development ask themselves difficult questions, tolerate a fair amount of discomfort as they turn inward for the answers, and value truth over fogginess when it comes to acknowledging the realities of their past. As a result of facing themselves fully and honestly, they have less to defend against or deny. They cultivate a sense of mastery over their internal world and, as a result, have more ease in living and live more easily in their own skin. They find their internal landscape interesting, even fascinating, because they understand that the hills and valleys are equally integral to who they are. They have no emotional investment in deceiving themselves or others with distortions of their value, either up or down. They appreciate the fact that an unobstructed view of themselves leads to a freer, more harmonious give-and-take between the outer world and the inner. They are not afraid to take the scenic tour of their inner surroundings while bearing in mind that like them, everyone else is navigating similarly complex terrain while roaming around in the dark. In understanding this, they demonstrate an awareness that we are all doing the best we can as we make our way around our psychic homelands.

Taking an actionable step toward shrinking the authenticity gap begins by going straight into it, but not before cultivating enough *self-regard*. You'll need this first, trust me, the way a marathon runner needs carbs for fuel and to replenish energy once the finish line is crossed. Self-regard is found, oddly enough, by exploring where and how it was first lost.

# Self-Regard

In my clinical practice, I have witnessed one sobering truth again and again: we do not get what we want; we get what we feel we deserve. I have watched my clients employ all sorts of strategies in order to meet big life goals and make dreams come true. Some have been successful. Most have not. Not for lack of intelligence, or talent, or grit, but more from some invisible drag on their wings. I have watched people struggle in their professional lives, in their love lives, and most painfully in their heads, as they've permitted me access to the deepest, most raw inner vision of themselves. I have heard their critical voices. Some were relentlessly harsh. Some were unreasonable. Too many were merciless, cruel. This got me thinking about why so many of us treat ourselves so terribly despite goals, desires, dreams. Self-regard, the consideration one has for oneself, cannot be built on a foundation of self-hatred. Any attempt to do so will simply not stick.

I have found that the odds were fairly high that repression of emotions was a prominent feature of growing up. A little girl afraid to go to school may have been told sharply by her mother, "Stop your nonsense. You're not afraid." A little boy who, through tears, told his father he was mocked at school may have heard, "What's wrong with you? I didn't raise a girl." Perhaps another child asked her parents if they would be attending her upcoming school play. They may have replied in an irritated tone, "And miss work? Who's going to pay the bills around here? You?"

Or maybe in your own life, your family suffered a loss when you were young and has never been the same since. Maybe you became enlisted in the role of caretaker to your grieving mom or dad, which required you to be a big girl or boy prematurely. If so, you assumed the role of adult, had overwhelming responsibilities and no one to lean on. In an emotional sense, you raised yourself. In time, you believed you didn't need anyone and to prove it, you sacrificed your needs. You shut them down. This tactical maneuver became the primary (and logical) means by which you dealt with the fact that no one was emotionally there for you, anyway. Maintaining a stance of fierce independence was likely how you closed yourself off from the hope (and crushing disappointment) that maybe someone would be there for you. Since your family's devastating loss, perhaps *you've* never been the same. There are countless variations of these scenarios, almost as many as there are individuals who survived imperfect childhoods.

Emotionally punitive or emotionally distant parents often produce a similar type of child, both by direct communication and by the examples set. Even if one has the intention of being 180 degrees different from his or her parent, simply being on the receiving end of punishment, unpredictability, withholding, self-absorption, or remoteness is enough for the child to absorb these unwanted traits and mimic them to some extent in adulthood. Conversely, a child may succeed at growing up to be the opposite of the parent, but this may paradoxically place her at risk for simply becoming the other side of the parental coin. For example, if one was raised by an excessively needy, self-absorbed parent, she may later grow up to loathe and disown the trait of neediness. As a result, she might later reject any semblance of neediness or dependency in herself, finding comfort in an airtight persona of extreme self-sufficiency and invulnerability. This is likely to make her feel secure and confident, but her impenetrable self-reliance may result in a barrier to intimacy. Others may find it difficult to get close to her, or she may not allow herself to receive from others. It may be an automatic unconscious reaction for her to equate intimacy with the memory of being in a one-sided relationship in which her needs were not only ignored, she was put in the impossibly frustrating position of satisfying the needs of a parent who was at once demanding and insatiable. Understandably, she views opening up emotionally as placing herself in jeopardy of being in the same impossible position all over again.

The astute child quickly learns what to do in order to navigate such rocky terrain: what is acceptable behavior and what isn't, what to say and what not to say, what to ask for and what not to expect. The child logically concludes that expressing feelings is wrong and futile. Before long, he or she figures out that denying these feelings is what must be done to stay on the parents' good side, avoid their criticism, earn their approval, or dodge their demands.

In instances where the parent may be limited or compromised due to grief, illness, immaturity, or poor mental health, the child may try to take care of the parent to preserve whatever capabilities exist in the parent's reserve. The child perceives, often rightly, that fortifying the parent by cheering a depressed mother, for instance, or supporting a fragile father, or being a confidant to a dependent caregiver is the best way to get the most of what the adult in charge has to offer. Okay, costly enough. What follows is at the core of many of my clients' unhappiness. It illustrates where and how self-regard is stolen.

On a psychological level, the child who was raised in such circumstances, however unintended any damage may have been, begins to no longer recognize or acknowledge his own feelings. Having been met with parental wrath, indifference, dismissal, emotional deafness, unavailability, or even well-intentioned but harsh correction, the child has no appropriate outlet nor receives comfort for his experience. His feelings are essentially denied by the only people who can, and should, validate them. By failing to provide the deserved validation, the parents end up *invalidating* their child's emotional experience. This response becomes internalized in the child's "download," and a powerful and fundamental lesson is learned, one that will last a lifetime: don't feel, because if you do, it will not go well.

The next thing that happens is on the physical level. The child literally tenses his body to brace against the emotional impact of his parents' disavowal so as to numb some of its effects. Eventually, this muscular constriction is used to force out the visceral experience of the unwanted feeling altogether. The child literally closes in on himself physically to tighten, that is to say, *control* the experience, preventing it from coming into conscious recognition. The physical tension itself becomes a defense mechanism. This bears repeating: the physical, muscular constriction becomes the way the child protects himself by preventing uncomfortable, confusing, or painful emotions from registering in the body as physical sensations.

The adult version of this can be seen in sessions where clients constrict their muscles without awareness that they are doing it as they recall something that is perceived as threatening: a painful memory or memory fragment, an intimidating interaction, or unnerving event. In an unconscious effort to short-circuit the physical sensations generated by the uncomfortable subject they are talking about, they might tense one of their ankles, for example, flexing it to an almost 90-degree angle. This is a reflex meant to literally force the feeling out of their body. Other clients, for example, without any conscious connection to what their hands are doing, tell an anger-laden story in a flat manner while making clenched fists or claw-like gesticulations—as if their body is telling one story while their words tell another, as if brain and body are not sharing a common set of facts.

Still others employ more private means of fighting off emerging feelings by clenching their jaw, squeezing their abdominal muscles, contracting their sphincter, holding their breath, or prolonging their eye blinks to blank out a surfacing emotion. None of this happens by conscious choice but by unconscious necessity. All these examples are signs that the action of self-alienation is taking place in exactly that moment. By repeatedly denying her true feelings, talking herself out of her own often correct appraisal of reality and rejecting her own truthful experience, the child-turned-adult is demonstrating the deeply ingrained coping pattern of dissociation.

For the child who has done this, the maturational process cannot help but be stunted. A significant degree of her personality will take shape largely around early, key emotional experiences. Those experiences may be distinct, traumatic events, such as a house fire, a sibling's injury, a parent's sickness or death, or a natural disaster. Other experiences may center around ongoing, smaller, and more subtle psychic hurts—micro-traumas—in which relatively mild or vague occurrences accumulate over time such as a home environment that was depressing, chaotic, unpredictable, grief-laden, anxious, or rigid. In either case, lacking the knowledge to fully understand her own needs and being incapable of comprehending her family's dynamics, the child's experience is overwhelming and confusing. She can easily think that she is the cause of her family's unhappiness. To maintain a certain equilibrium and function normally, she concludes that she must stay away from her inner state, that to feel it is painfully intolerable. The profound discomfort and fear are held in and not permitted their natural release. By sheer unconscious will, painful and upsetting emotions are not acknowledged, and the pathways by which these emotions are experienced—bodily sensations—are blocked. Having no outlet, they become stuck in her body, lodged within the tension and constriction of her muscles. Then to lessen the intensity of her body's discomfort, she may enter an even deeper emotional state of detachment. This occurs when one disconnects from one's inner self, feeling "divorced" from bodily sensations, emotions, feelings, and behaviors almost as if they belong to someone else. This can leave these individuals feeling hazy or "unreal," with a sense that something is missing within them. Some describe themselves as walking around behind a veil or a see-through curtain, a "plexiglass wall," as one client described, causing them to feel as though they are dissociated from themselves and distant from others. They can see out into the world but are not emotionally touched by it. This is a profoundly difficult way to get through life.

A lifelong pattern will emerge whenever such an individual is triggered by a feeling she does not want to feel. It will surface not only in the exact moment the unwanted feeling arises but will be absorbed into her personality as a mainstay of surviving life itself. This pattern will develop into a generalized emotional "life shield" that she will unconsciously use to deflect further pain and overwhelming aloneness. Giving up this shield, she believes, will lead to certain danger. She is convinced that 1) it is not safe to rely on anyone but herself, 2) it is dangerous to feel vulnerable, and 3) her feelings neither affect the outcome of a situation nor matter, and therefore neither does she.

With all this self-censoring going on in the child's unconscious mind during the course of her young life, one wonders how much of her true self is left for a healthy adulthood. To what extent are we also out of touch with our real self, and what does this say about the self we show to the world? This question gets to the heart of why I and so many others choose this work.

If asked what in my view is the main objective of psychotherapy, i.e., what it is that my clients and I are trying to accomplish together, I would say, wholeheartedly, it is to 1) help them come face-to-face with their hidden and therefore unknown selves, and 2) expand their willingness to embrace what they discover about themselves along the way, in essence, to help them improve their relationship with themselves. The more they, and indeed all of us, can use the "I" of us, our consciousness, to accept the truth about the rest of us, the more we can incorporate the parts of ourselves into a unified whole. Only when we can hold the entire range of notes in our emotional octave by willingly embracing the totality of who we are: the good, the bad, and perhaps most especially what we perceive as the ugly, will we be able to enjoy the symphony of self-acceptance and the accompaniment of greater acceptance of others. Only then can we live securely in our own skin. Without self-validation, we remain forever at the mercy of outside forces and circumstances, unable to masterfully direct the course of our own lives. We continue to bob along, adrift, longing for someone or something to rescue us from our own self-judgment.

Going through life overly concerned with being saved, pleasing others, sidestepping others' wrath, or trying to get others to meet our needs can lead to a basic conflict with whether we live for ourselves or for others:

"Do I live my life based on my own personal, mature beliefs, or do I ignore my convictions so that others will accept me?"

"Do I make decisions in my life based on what I think, feel and desire, or am I unclear of what it is that I even want?"

"Have I become so used to not making waves that I've swallowed my voice entirely?"

"Will I be overwhelmed by my emotions if I truly acknowledge some of the things I've been through?"

These were the type of questions asked by several of my clients in just one week alone. They may not have all used the same words to express their concerns, but their reflections were clear examples of just how pervasive and troubling giving up on the "self" really is.

Giving up our sense of self-determination, the process by which we control our own lives, strips us of the ability to live the life that we were meant to live. The emotional discomfort that surfaces when we don't live as the competent adult we know ourselves to be is both painful and demoralizing. Living in this manner prevents us from discovering our true self and jeopardizes the areas of our lives that are most important to us. Clinging to this approach and to the unchallenged beliefs that were handed down to us by our caretakers, themselves well-meaning but flawed human beings, keeps us stuck.

In other words, we are stuck in life not because anyone or anything is holding us prisoner, but because we are holding onto beliefs that are limiting and restrictive, too afraid or too uninspired to let them go.

Seeing the problem of stuckness as a matter of actively *holding on* from the inside rather than passively *being forced* from the outside allows more room to experiment with newer, more self-validating perspectives.

When we can give ourselves permission to let go of what other people think of us long enough to own our story, our truth, and our experience, we gain deeper access to our self-respect. Without question, it is the ability to honor the reality of our past that births and then nurtures our sense of worthiness. When we do, we give ourselves the powerful message that we are worth our own recognition. Conversely, spending a lifetime trying to distance ourselves from the parts of our lives that don't square up with who we think we're supposed to be places us outside our reality. We try to earn our value by playing to an audience to whom we audition, acquiesce, appeal, and apologize. We desperately twist ourselves into the proverbial pretzel. We'll be loved, "if only." Twist, wait, twist, wait, twist . . .

This "if only" way of living is extremely seductive because our mind always thinks we are merely one approval or accomplishment short of our goal, the goal of being regarded as a valuable person. One more. Maybe this time. Maybe next time. This makes me think of casinos. "Maybe if I spend this dollar or that hundred or that thousand, I'll hit the jackpot on the next spin of the wheel or roll of the dice. I can't walk away. What if the next time is it—the one I've been waiting for?" We all get hooked into playing "Wheel of Misfortune."

Our misguided belief system is the currency that keeps us in the game.

My clients demonstrate a simple fact every day through their earnest but futile attempts at looking for worthiness in all the wrong places: worthiness is not earned. It simply cannot be earned. It is something that is realized from the inside, not granted from the outside. It is not scored by judges, like on *Dancing With the Stars*. There is no golden buzzer, regardless of how great the performance. No one's worthiness is voted off, regardless of how poor the performance. Accolades don't provide it, failures don't forfeit it. In a literal sense, you had as much to do with its onset as you did with determining your eye color. Worthiness is on your humanity's DNA. It is on everyone's. The work was done for you before you got here. It predates and outlasts circumstances and opportunity, although from a socioeconomic point of view, circumstance and opportunity affect the degree to which self-worth will be actualized.

Each of us has it. Each of us *is* it. The fact that we don't know or have forgotten this is the crux of most of our problems. We misread *not knowing* we're worthy for *believing we're not worthy*. There is a big difference between the two. Then to prove ourselves correct (we humans love to be right), we fly as if led by some heat-seeking missile, straight toward those people and situations that seem to confirm our belief. Nothing confirms feeling unworthy faster than pursuing emotionally unavailable people, for instance. Despite this, we try to be happy. No wonder things aren't working out.

Along the way, in the midst of our heat-seeking, we tend to make assumptions about other heat seekers. We see their fancy facades and conclude that it is their adornments that make them worthy beings. None of us has X-ray vision. It is impossible to know anyone else's inner experience, impossible to know whether they are among the lucky or enlightened few who have embraced their innate value or whether they are heeding the messages in this book along with the rest of us. Either way, our addiction to comparison is our greatest underminer. We seem hell-bent on glorifying what we see in others while shining a shame spotlight on what we see in ourselves.

Imagine what would happen if you invited (or dared) yourself to curb your habit for comparison. But how? I'm going to suggest that you start by looking inward with as much curiosity as you look outward toward others. I'm going to suggest that you become extremely interested in yourself.

## Self-Interest

Let's face it. Selflessness is considered a virtue, while selfishness is practically a felony. Isn't it true that one of the worst insults that can be leveled against us is that we are behaving selfishly? Are you concerned that too much focusing on your inner thoughts and feelings means that you are overly wrapped up in yourself? Too egotistical? Too self-absorbed?

If so, you can relax. There is such a thing as healthy selfishness or what author and self-esteem expert, Nathaniel Branden, calls "enlightened self-interest." It is characterized as neither a disregard for others nor a self-serving, head-swelling endeavor for you. The work of Nathaniel Branden has significantly influenced my own work, particularly when it comes to helping clients grow in their self-esteem.

In this context, enlightened self-interest means purposefully allowing your "aware self" to gather more information about the rest of you. It includes the development of an important skill known as mindfulness, the ability to bring your sensory awareness to whatever is going on within you in any given moment. Mindfulness is the skill that will reorient your attention toward, rather than away from your inner self.

Developing this skill will go a long way toward helping you inhabit your body, the place where emotions are experienced in the form of feelings. You will need this ability, most importantly, because if you hope to unstick yourself from negative, long-standing patterns, you need to catch yourself in the act of turning your decision-making over to unexamined impulses and reflexive reactions. Recognizing the exact moment in which you steer away from your personal truth is the only real window for change. If this is a new skill for you, don't worry, it is easier to develop than you think. All you need is your willingness and some practice. I estimate, anecdotally, that becoming proficient in this one area has allowed my clients to make their biggest leap toward progress, perhaps by as much as 50 percent.

Perhaps you consider "thinking about yourself" a waste of time, hardly a productive endeavor. After all, you have better things to do than contemplate your inner state, don't you?

Actually, you don't. An unexamined self is a little like a loose cannon: powerful but messy. The time invested in the journey of self-discovery is time well spent. Self-understanding is not a required skill for human functioning, but it *is* a necessary one for successful *adult* functioning. If you are willing to learn the skill of mindfulness and understand the anatomy of your divided self, you can unquestionably look forward to unsticking yourself from stubborn and stifling patterns. You will not only improve your relationship with yourself, which just may be one of the most important things you will ever do, you will improve the health of every relationship of which you are a part.

We will focus more on mindfulness later in these pages. For now, let us get back to what is arguably the most potent barrier to self-acceptance, self-love, and peace of mind. It contains the root of many of our issues including self-sabotage, addiction, failed relationships, self-defeating behavior, loneliness, and emptiness.

## Not Good Enough

"Not good enough" is not an official diagnosis, disability, or disadvantage. You won't find it in the DSM-V, the go-to compendium of emotional disorders used by mental health professionals to identify psychiatric disorders. If you suffer from it, there are no special tags to hang from your car mirror to indicate that you may be disabled by it, nor are there employment policies that will excuse you from work while you recuperate from it. Insurance companies don't cover it, and chances are, most good doctors fail to recognize it.

Although virtually undetectable in its latent form, this almost endemic condition can be seen in the outward signs and symptoms of many debilitating and baffling problems: emotional paralysis, despite "knowing what to do," self-sabotage, chaotic and cluttered living, perfectionism, low self-esteem, procrastination, insomnia, food issues, addictions. The list goes on. Furthermore, despite its widespread nature, no one talks about it, few realize they suffer from it, and almost no one seeks help for it, directly. The "not good enough disorder" is one of the worst-kept secrets in our American culture, and it is hiding in plain sight.

How do you know if you're suffering from "I'm not good enough"? Here are some key signs:

- You have a subtle, gnawing feeling that you don't measure up to others.
- No matter how hard you try, you feel that your best often falls short.
- You feel that you are only as good as your last accomplishment.
- You crave validation, and when you don't get it, you feel deflated.
- You constantly compare yourself to others.
- You play down your accomplishments.
- You feel uncomfortable accepting compliments.
- You put yourself and your needs last.
- You often come up short with time, rest, and money.
- You feel like a child in a world full of adults.
- You overdo to compensate for feeling inadequate or "less than."
- You often find yourself feeling envious of others.
- You seldom ask for what you need.
- You are not sure of what you need.
- You don't like feeling as though you even have needs.
- You people-please.
- You avoid confrontation.
- You don't feel that you have the same rights as others.
- You struggle to find your voice.
- You feel that your opinions don't count.

- You are vaguely aware of an inner void and do almost anything to avoid feeling it.
- You find yourself compelled to do things such as overeat, procrastinate, or numb out, even though you want to stop.
- You say you're "fine" all the time, regardless of what is going on in your day.
- You agree with others just to keep the peace, avoid making waves or risking anyone's anger or displeasure.
- You cry easily, especially when you feel frustrated.
- You find it hard to cry.
- You speak in a loud tone of voice.
- You speak in a barely audible tone of voice.
- You behave in a way that garners a lot of attention.
- You behave in a way that almost makes you invisible.
- You are prone to act aggressively.
- You tend to act passively.
- You don't know how to take care of yourself emotionally.
- You refuse to take care of yourself emotionally.
- You tend to be a rescuer.
- You aren't sure how to rescue yourself.

This list is not exhaustive. I could have easily included many more signs. If you're thinking that what did make the list describes you and just about everyone you know, take heart. As I said earlier, the "not good enough disorder" is a widespread and encompassing phenomenon. How is it, why is it, that so many of us are afflicted by this insidious and pervasive disregard for our genuine nature, our tender hearts, our true selves? To understand this, we must first understand authenticity.

The word *authentic* happens to be one of my favorite words. Probably because it is such an important word, a truth-teller sort of word, a bottom-line sort of word. Dictionaries define authentic as "not false or copied; genuine; real; with an origin supported by unquestionable evidence; authenticated; verified; representing one's true nature or beliefs; true to oneself; reliable; trustworthy."

In the previous section, we heard some of the things parents say to their children in the interest of teaching them to behave in an "acceptable" manner, to have "proper" expectations, and to conform to the "rules" of the home at times so as not to stress the caregivers. To this end, caregivers exercise their authority to shape the way children think. While this may seem almost too obvious to mention, what is fascinating to explore is the flood of unseen phenomena that occur in the mind, body, and spirit of a young person who, in an effort to find acceptance from caregivers, slips into the early throes of self-alienation.

As infants grow into their very early childhood, they learn that they are separate from their primary caregivers. They begin to experience their emotions as their own. Thus they take an initial and crucial step into selfhood. If the environment in which they develop is a nurturing one and their emerging individuality is supported and validated, chances for a healthy autonomy are increased greatly. If on the other hand the familial atmosphere is unstable, rigid, chaotic, sterile, or otherwise not conducive to facilitating the child's unique maturation, chances for repression of a true self are high. Like a flower that bends toward the sunlight to blossom, children's highest expression of their inborn nature is nourished and sustained in the light of their parents' acceptance of who they are. Working with people in psychotherapy and clinical coaching, I have many opportunities to witness the tragic consequences of selves that feel unentitled to fully inhabit the skin they live in, individuals who feel they must do as they have always done and disown the very heart of who they know themselves to be. When this occurs, people become symptomatic. I see their symptoms as the manifestations of an ill-fated existence.

To be alienated from the self is to live in an inauthentic manner, to be insufficiently conscious of one's body, one's needs, wants, emotions, values, actions, reactions, capacities, and limitations. The alienated self lives as a virtual stranger to itself, moving through life disconnected from internal gauges, thereby becoming overly dependent on cues from others.

Self-alienated individuals may rely on others to tell them what to think, what to feel, what is acceptable to express, what is appropriate, what is not. At a minimum, the cost of self-alienation and its direct consequence—inauthenticity—is steep. It can easily leave one feeling unprepared for adulthood, forever childlike in an over-reliance on other, more "knowledgeable" adults and extraordinarily frustrated for reasons that are not understood by the conscious mind.

When we are unaware of our needs and wants, we face life without the compass necessary to navigate them. We remain directionless, adrift, and without a course to follow. We remain stuck. In this state, time seems to pass us by. We renew our promises to get moving again, in our relationships, in our businesses, and in our own attitudes toward life, but inexplicably we stand still.

## CHAPTER 4

# Another Year

Another year. Hell, another decade.

"I'm stuck."

We say it defensively, desperately, despairingly. It's our excuse, our mantra, our name tag.

"I'm really stuck."

It's what we say when we can't get traction. When we spin our wheels, going fast and in circles, gaining little ground. Gaining, instead, weight, debt, stress, loneliness, boredom, self-loathing.

"I'm stuck."

It's what we mean even when we call stuckness by its other names, hoping to peel it off ourselves and toss it elsewhere. "They won't let me." "They'll criticize me." "They'll judge me."

"I'm hopelessly stuck."

It's the place where we're frozen, shame and fear halting us, mid-step. "I'm paralyzed, trapped."

"I'm stuck feeling stuck."

It's the view we have of ourselves, beneath our facades and behind our walls: I'm not good enough.

Being stuck is no joke. Sure, there are a million other maladies that seem more crippling, and indeed are. Yet, as we have begun to see, if you're emotionally stuck, you know it. You know it by the chronic setbacks in your productivity. You see it in your playing it safe, and small. You recognize it by the critical voice in your head that yanks you away from your potential and hurls you back to square one, time after time.

If you know the frustration of being stuck, you are familiar with the sense that your behavior and your self-esteem are somehow being hijacked. You have seen your determination become undone and your dreams, despite your effort, fail to become reality. As if immune to every anti-stuck promise you make, every vow to call forth willpower and grit, stagnation, it seems, wins out. What's more, you know how incredibly stubborn stuckness can be. The more you fight it, the harder it fights back. It devours your time when you're looking the other way, making to-do lists and thinking up more ways to defeat it. In the blink of an eye, whole years pass you by. Suddenly, it's another summer.

Depressing, isn't it?

The truth is you may not be stuck in all areas of your life. You may do better in some than in others. For instance, you may excel at your job, but your social life is almost nonexistent. Or your relationship is going well, but your finances are disastrous. You've gotten your clutter under control, but your drinking has picked up. You work on your marriage but neglect your health.

You take care of one problem, and another problem pops up. It's emotional Whack-A-Mole.

No one sets out to be negative. No one purposely trips up in a relationship or at work. No one consciously chooses to gain weight when she knows exactly how to eat healthfully. No one decides to date unavailable people.

And yet we do.

How does this happen, and why? What is the reason smart, capable people get in their own way, forfeit their authenticity, and fail to live up to their potential? Or are run by behavior patterns that not only don't serve them but cause them pain? The answer will surprise you. In fact, you may even reject it at first.

We are all aware of those sneering, belittling things we say to ourselves and those behaviors that we know slip us up, such as procrastinating, forgetting, or getting caught up in trying to be perfect. The examples are many: we may set the alarm incorrectly for that job interview we were finally granted, or misplace our car keys, making us late for the important meeting we requested with the boss. We may become overly picky with new people we date, finding irredeemable fault with each one, or have a temper tantrum in front of our new romantic partner just as things seem to be taking off. In business, we might delay sending the email to that influential person we met at the networking event who could potentially boost our bottom line. Of even greater consequence, we may do things like stay in an unhealthy relationship way too long or overlook the obvious red flags when someone is treating us poorly.

Most of us are unaware, however, that these seemingly isolated behaviors are just the tip of a self-perpetuating iceberg—merely glimpses of a larger, well-hidden foe that lies deep within each of us, influencing our choices, and derailing our happiness.

The reason we become stuck, can't move forward, and end up sabotaging our success and happiness in life is because there is a hidden benefit to doing so, an underlying advantage to sidelining our success. It may be surprising to learn that the hidden cause of our self-defeat is an unrecognized attempt to solve a problem. There is what therapists refer to as a "secondary gain" to developing and maintaining undesirable behavior patterns. A secondary gain is a hidden benefit that often accompanies unwanted behavior. These hidden benefits satisfy our need to keep ourselves emotionally safe in whatever way we deem necessary.

Monica, a woman in her early thirties, for example, once told me she could never date a man who wore a suit, even though she very much wanted to meet a financially successful businessman. When I asked her to tell me more, it was clear that she tended to date men her age who were adolescent in nature. They bounced from job to job, rebelled against authority, were irresponsible with money, and consistently put their own needs above her's and everyone else's. Though she complains about these men and laments her chronic loneliness, a closer look reveals that she does not feel like a grown woman in her own right, and therefore backs away from men whom she perceives as adults: "I wouldn't know how to relate to a man who is in charge of his life, an established, successful man. And why would someone like that want to date me?"

To this client, a smart, attractive woman with two master's degrees, the man in a suit seems like too much of an adult and represents everything she is not. Because she inwardly feels like a much younger version of herself, she unconsciously gravitates toward an emotionally younger man, someone who is her emotional and energetic equal, all the while wondering why her relationships do not work out.

The secondary gain of selecting this type of man is that

she gets to feel "safe" within the bounds of her diminished self-esteem. To allow herself to pair up with someone whom she perceives as more adult would mean she runs the risk of feeling highly uncomfortable in his company: overwhelmed, intimidated, and emotionally dwarfed. She unintentionally (but deliberately in her unconscious mind) sabotages her chances of being in a mature and fulfilling relationship in exchange for maintaining her psychological equilibrium. Though she is lonely, frustrated, and upset with the men she dates, she is destined to repeat this pattern with whom she avoids and whom she pursues. There isn't a dating app on the planet that can bypass, override, or penetrate her fearful mindset. The men she swipes right on and goes out with are perfect matches for her shrinking self-esteem.

The main reason we too get in our own way and unintentionally sabotage our success and happiness is because we are trying to protect ourselves in some way. We hold on to problematic behavior patterns in effect because we think that letting them go places us at risk for major discomfort or to feel hurt in some way. Our so-called negative behavior and self-defeating programming are ways in which we shield ourselves from feeling vulnerable and exposed.

"How can that be?" you ask. "Protect myself from what!? I really do want to be able to move forward in my life. Besides, if I am really trying to protect myself, why do I feel so frustrated? Shouldn't my 'protection' make me feel better, happier?"

See, I told you.

It's all right. Your reaction is perfectly understandable. You feel this way because it is your conscious mind that is motivated to move ahead and make your dreams a reality;

your conscious self that wants to live a happy, authentic, and meaningful life. Everything in your awareness signals a green light to move forward.

The Problem?

Part of the problem is that the problem is not where you think it is. The problem does not exist in your conscious awareness at all but resides somewhere else entirely. Until you know exactly where to look, finding the real root of your frustration will elude you.

The place to look for answers is in your subconscious mind. Looking to your conscious mind for why you sabotage your happiness is like traveling west looking for a sunrise. No matter how hard you try to find it, the sunrise is still behind you, in the opposite direction. If you want to see where the sun is rising and experience it in all its purples and fuchsias and golds, you must first turn around.

## Your Emotional Compass

Looking deeper, the reason we pit ourselves against our own thoughts and best interests is because our conscious and unconscious selves have competing agendas. This may seem surprising, but it's true. The part of us that wants to succeed and be happy is at odds with the part determined to keep us right where we are. When we are close to reaching important goals, for instance, goals that mean a great deal to us or make promises to ourselves but then habitually blow it right before we cross the finish line (we lose interest, get distracted, shut down, procrastinate, hit the fridge, get tied up with being perfect, drink, socialize, or otherwise avoid bringing things to completion), we can be sure that something within us is blocking our success. Our stuckness is not happening by accident although it appears that it is.

This anti-self behavior is a glimpse into the contradictory nature that exists within each one of us, the deep but unseen conflict that leaves us at cross purposes with our deepest, most heartfelt desires.

## CHAPTER 5

# Who Needs Enemies When We've Got Ourselves?

The disparity between our competing selves, between our determined selves and our stuck selves, between our good and our bad, our weak and our strong, our smart and not so smart selves, is nothing new. Most of us know what to do and not do, but we rebel against our own best advice.

This contradictory and dual nature of the human condition has been studied and explored by great minds for centuries. Still this topic continues to confound us. Watching our dreams come crashing down as we try to move forward, hampered by our own behavior—sometimes curious, sometimes baffling, sometimes utterly stupid—causing hurt not only to ourselves but often to the people we love, is one of the saddest things we can do to ourselves.

And yet this behavior is everywhere. We see it in the headlines and in our news feed on an almost daily basis. You've no doubt noticed the steady stream of accomplished and often respected individuals who foul up their lives when they could otherwise have it all. It is staggering. The cringe-worthy and profoundly self-defeating behavior of numerous politicians, entertainers, sports figures, Hollywood moguls, financiers, clergy, etc., has many of us aghast as we witness the self-inflicted teardown of their success. With a mixture of disapproval, contempt, disgust, and pity, we say, "Who could possibly be so self-destructive? So dumb? So cruel? So blindly entitled? Those foolish individuals, right? What's wrong with them?"

Furthermore, in the privacy of our mind we may even add, "Hey, I may not be perfect, but I could never do anything even close to what they've done. I may be bad, but at least I'm not that bad!" What a relief it is to our conscious mind that we're not that! Sure, maybe in moments of extreme anger or frustration or desperation, any one of us could do things or behave in uncharacteristic ways, but the truth is when it comes to us, our responses feel justified. We think of ourselves as a patient person, don't we? However, the driver who cut us off on the road this morning deserves all our wrath (cursing and revenge fantasies). We see ourselves as generous. Yet that extraordinarily large supply of water and food we piled in our grocery cart when the superstorm was predicted . . . well, we might need it. Hurry! Others will just have to deal with it and figure it out for themselves. We're the first to celebrate the accomplishments of others, but that bonus we sheepishly accepted for the clever idea that really belonged to a coworker, well, "She's given kudos all the time. It was finally my turn."

Interestingly, when we take more than our fair share of things, behave selfishly, unleash disproportionate rage toward someone, or act irrationally, we display a version of the very behaviors we despise in others. When it comes to us however, those behaviors don't feel selfish or aggressive; they feel normal, a handy double standard offered by our unconscious mind in order to rationalize the actions of our conscious selves. The result: a mindset that can make it seem as though there is a "good" us and a "bad" them. This split is at the heart of why we turn against ourselves. If we can deny what we judge negatively in ourselves, we remain locked into an imbalanced view of our true nature. We artificially live in the illusion that we are completely one way or another, when in fact we are both. We are good *and* bad.

The stark truth is that each of us is generous and selfish, patient, and aggressive, selfless, and greedy. Each of us carries the potential to be all things, depending on the circumstances. No one is strictly one way or the other. To believe otherwise is to forever defend against those parts of ourselves which we perceive as bad. We erect a psychological wall between the good and bad in ourselves, and we use that same wall to divide the good us from the bad them. The upside of this is that we are spared the discomfort of delving into certain uncomfortable truths, such as the aching things we've been through, the way we feel toward those who may have failed or disappointed us, cheated or abandoned us. The downside is that by not facing these truths, we remain at a loss for how to constructively handle them. This binary perspective frames the way we look at our emotions and causes us to categorize life's experiences into narrow pigeonholes of black or white, good, or bad, all or nothing, right or wrong.

How many times have you had similar "me vs. them" thoughts?

I know I have, and often. That is until I learned to better understand the riddle of our duality.

# Me and My Shadow

The darker side of the human psyche, coined the "shadow" by Swiss psychologist Carl Jung, is at the root of this two-fold mindset and drives every act of undoing and self-defeat we commit. It doesn't stem from the parts of ourselves that we like or feel good about. Instead it arises from the depths of our shame, self-loathing, and fear, and thrives ironically on our denial of its very existence. This is worth repeating: *The darker side of our consciousness lives and thrives in our very denial of it.* The more oblivious we are to it, the stronger it becomes. Something is hardwired into our humanness that causes us to revolt against our most privately held vulnerability, against the parts of ourselves we fear will get us rejected, thrown away, or ignored. Simply put, we are compelled to disown what we judge to be "bad."

Why? It is an evolutionary imperative that we belong to a social group or "tribe." Belonging to a larger whole was essential to survival: people hunted and cooked in groups, shared the workload, and protected one another. Not only were they trying to ensure their own survival, but all members of the tribe were invested in each other's successful outcome because everyone played an important role in the survival of the entire group. If one lost standing in the tribe, that individual's literal survival was in jeopardy since the ability to stay alive on one's own was considerably difficult.

Although in Western culture we no longer rely on tribes in the way we once did, there remains a fundamental need to "belong," to ensure psychological and social connection. There is a large body of evidence that suggests people are happier and healthier when they experience social belonging.

Social exclusion, on the other hand, has been found to influence us humans in painful ways emotionally, cognitively, and behaviorally. To avoid these consequences, we developed specific tactics and behaviors, the sole functions of which are to prevent rejection and promote inclusion.

One of the foremost among these is the gradual chipping away of any aspect of ourselves which we feel could get a "thumbs down" from our "tribe," whomever they may be. We are so intent on reading the approval signs from others that we instantaneously size up their reactions and adjust our responses accordingly. Our default reaction is to reject in ourselves (censor, negate, downplay, hide) that which we perceive is displeasing to others. Better we do the rejecting, we think, then have someone else do it to us first. Too sheepish and afraid to offer our opinion, ask for help, take risks, disagree, or otherwise assert ourselves, we swallow our genuineness and our voice, and we swallow hard.

This means that in warding off rejection from others, we send ourselves straight into rejection of ourselves in the most insidious of ways. The denial of our most authentic nature, over time, results in a virtual estrangement from the truth of our deepest selves. We become the person we think we are supposed to be to win the approval and love of others. Eventually, we believe that the edited, censored version of ourselves is the real us and the disowned us no longer exists. Our identity becomes upside down and we are convinced that the way to belong is to keep it that way.

Our unconscious mind has an interesting way of achieving this by skewing the way we perceive ourselves and others. By taking our "bad" qualities and seeing them in others but not in ourselves, we trick ourselves into believing that others are the carriers of shadowy negativity while we are not. This mind trick of projection is the "how to" mechanism by which we convince ourselves we are not undesirable or bad. "They" are the ones who are greedy, arrogant, jealous, rageful, judgmental, needy, over-reactive, petty, sneaky, manipulative, critical, gossipy, controlling, dishonest, aggressive, cold, unfeeling, and so on. Us? We're pretty nice.

I recall an instance some years back, before I knew very much about shadow work, when I was in a large upscale grocery market in New York City. I decided to go to the salad bar. While choosing my selections, I glanced up and noticed a woman standing directly across from me alongside a man whom I presumed to be her husband. She was about my age, attractive, stylishly dressed in NYC black chic, and accessorized with bold, trendy jewelry. I admired her look. We made split-second eye contact before looking away. In the next moment, she asked her husband in a rather loud tone of voice whether he preferred the crab legs or the shrimp salad wherein they proceeded to nonchalantly chow down a whole dinner for two right from the salad bar! No container, no utensils, just dipping into the various trays of food with their fingers. A little shrimp salad followed by some crab legs topped off with some melon and a few grapes.

I stared incredulously and probably conspicuously for the minute or two that this couple appeared to graze down the entire length of the salad bar. I felt a surge of anger well up in me from my solar plexus like a blowtorch. I wanted to scream at them. "How dare you be so arrogant! So entitled! So selfish!" I wanted to aim my mental blowtorch directly at them so much so that for the next few minutes I followed them through the store, trailing them up and down the aisles as I rehearsed what I would say to them. I practiced my insults. I honed exactly how I intended to shame her. Although I'm not a big fan of reporting people to higher-ups, you can be sure I was headed straight to the management once I made my confrontation move. I felt dizzy with anger over her blatant sense of entitlement, and I couldn't wait to tell her so. Though this type of reaction wasn't my typical *modus operandi*, I was loaded for bear and all in.

. . . Another minute went by.

Well, I never did confront the couple. (I ditched them in the soup aisle, too riled up to see what damage they might have done there.) I took a few moments to cool the white-hot anger I was feeling. "Deep breaths. 10, 9, 8, . . . ," before continuing.

The truth, as I came to realize it, was that I was uncomfortable with my level of anger. The revenge fantasy in my mind played like a pinball machine, pinging me first to relief, then to shame, then satisfaction, then back to shame. The deeper truth is I feared that if I started to attack her verbally, I might not want to stop.

Something inside did stop me, and I'm glad that it did. I will admit that for months after, whenever I thought about her or passed a salad bar, I felt anger in my body. I told myself many times to just let it go. But the image and the feelings wouldn't leave.

I later understood the reasons for this. I learned that whenever we spot our disowned features in other people, we judge them harshly to distance ourselves from them. By railing against such features, characteristics, and behaviors, we "prove" that we are *anything but that*. It is a highly effective tactic that keeps our "unacceptable" and therefore *denied self* outside our awareness, and our *idealized self* front and center.

This defense mechanism is one of the most powerful strategies we have in our rejection-proof arsenal, and most people don't know they are using it. I certainly didn't.

One of the biggest consequences of relying on this mechanism is that we project onto others those behaviors and attributes that we believe are beneath us and thereby miss opportunities to face something in ourselves. When we do this, we inadvertently ignore deep facets of who we are. At the same time, we begin the buildup of internal pressure in our mind/body system that comes from trying to bury these aspects. Experienced in our body as tension and in our mind as strain, this cumulative and suppressed energy intensifies as we strive to ignore what we don't like about ourselves. Think about it, trying not to be something we already are requires some fancy mental footwork.

In her groundbreaking book, *The Shadow Effect*, coach, teacher, and consultant Debbie Ford brought widespread attention to this very phenomenon. Regarding the intensity that builds up when vital aspects of the self are ignored, Ms. Ford compares suppressing our truth to holding an inflated beach ball under water. It can only be done for so long before the ball "pops up and hits you right in the face and in the most inopportune times." (Ford, 2010). The more we disown ourselves and keep aspects of our humanness submerged, the more we increase the likelihood that what we have suppressed will catch up with us one day when we can no longer endure the pressure. This will likely show up as an inevitable blow-up, meltdown, unraveling, or collapse at some point in our lives. We can only suppress for so long. This is when most of my clients first call me. The beach ball effect, of which Ms. Ford writes, is "the cumulative heartbreak, devastation, self-sabotage and desperation that finally pierces the veil of suppression." As much as I wish my clients would phone sooner, before their beach ball pops back up, before they have the affair or turn a blind eye to obvious relationship problems, or let themselves run on empty for too long, or self-medicate with alcohol or shopping, I know that their "breakdowns" are actually the beginning of their breakthroughs.

How then do we join with the very aspects of ourselves that we have disowned until now? How do we begin to recognize our shadow in the first place?

About a year after the salad bar incident, I found myself at one of Debbie Ford's intensive workshops called the Shadow Process, a three-day experiential workshop on exactly this subject, the intense emotions that arise within each of us when certain people push our buttons and what happens when these emotions are either acted out or suppressed. During one of the exercises, Debbie (I feel like I can call her by her first name after revealing some very personal and shameful things, and receiving not a judgment but a warm, accepting hug) asked the participants to think of a person we despised. It could be someone we knew well or someone we had a chance encounter with. Bingo! She then asked us to list the qualities in that person we disliked most. Easy: arrogance, entitlement, and self-serving!

We were asked to consider the following questions. 1) What could possibly lead someone to behave in such a manner? 2) Is it possible that I possess these qualities deep down but are too ashamed to admit it? 3) Could I be in denial about my own ability to behave as the woman in the market did, *under the right circumstances*? 4) How might those traits, the ones I abhorred, potentially serve me if I were to use them consciously, in an awakened state?

After some resistance to these questions—I couldn't see anything redeeming arising from the salad bar qualities—I recalled the saying, "What we resist, persists." I hung in there, and eventually I began to feel awash with a few uncomfortable truths. Although I knew nothing of the woman's experience, I did ask myself if there were any circumstances under which I could see myself taking something that did not belong to me. Yes, if I felt desperate enough. Food? Absolutely, if I didn't know where my next meal was coming from. Then I pondered whether I had ever taken anything from anyone without their knowledge. More shame, but yes. I have taken people's time and attention. Once, I was mistakenly given too much change by a cashier at a big box store, and although I realized it, I said nothing. Instead, I rationalized that the company made millions and surely wouldn't miss my twenty dollars. And remember the earlier example of loading up a shopping cart when the threat of a big storm sends anxious shoppers to the grocery stores to stock up on food and supplies? In anticipation of Superstorm Sandy a few years ago, I bought more than my fair share of batteries, beyond what anyone could use in a lifetime, frankly too anxious and self-focused to think about anyone else's need. My benevolent-toward-others attitude, the same one I pride myself on, apparently goes out the window when I'm panicky about my roof blowing off. The shame hits keep coming. Fortunately, I remembered this during the early stages of the pandemic and resisted the impulse to amass huge quantities of toilet paper.

Shadow work is based on the understanding that we humans possess the seed for every human quality imaginable, and that every quality, every emotion, and every experience come bearing the seeds of great gifts. In her workshops, Debbie asks the audience her signature question, "What hidden gifts are contained in the qualities we judge as bad?"

If we were to turn our so-called negative qualities inside out, would we discover some benefit to their existence, some way in which they might serve us? The answer is an interesting yes. Take for example the quality of aggression. This is widely viewed as a negative trait, particularly so in women, still. What could be the "gift" contained in being aggressive?

Let's say you felt that someone was trying to take advantage of you in some way. Perhaps a contractor, business associate, salesperson, or service provider. You have made attempts to handle this in a calm, respectful manner, but nothing seemed to change. It might be time to call upon your bolder nature. Your capacity to be aggressive might be what is needed to protect yourself and establish clear boundaries. If you're unable to access this quality because you judge it as wrong, unattractive, or impolite, and therefore cut it off, you run the risk of being increasingly susceptible to others' aggression without a way to constructively deal with it. At the same time, if you often handle things aggressively right out of the gate because you view diplomacy or tactfulness as forms of weakness and therefore cut those qualities off in yourself, you will likely attract more aggression to you, as others will pick up on your edgy vibration and respond accordingly. Either way, over-valuing or under-valuing a trait can be the very thing that attracts more of it into your life.

Back to the salad bar qualities: Can arrogance and entitlement ever be helpful attributes? It's difficult to imagine that they could be. After all, their connotation is generally seen as negative and off-putting. However, if we ask ourselves, "What sort of person might behave that way?," we may come up with the following possibilities: a person who believes he or she is worthy of having what they desire, a person who feels he or she has certain rights and isn't afraid to live according to them, or a person who believes that their importance is equal to others. The other crucial questions to ask here are: Where in my life have I not been able to feel worthy of my desires? or When haven't I viewed myself as equal to others? If someone's behavior gets under our skin, if it brings out a disproportionate amount of anger in us, it very well may be because it echoes a suppressed urge to behave in a similar way, or it shines a light on a matching impulse within us that we don't want to admit.

The idea here isn't so much about the couple's actions at the salad bar, per se. Condoning or excusing their behavior is less the issue than understanding the intensity of my own reaction. The objectionable behavior we see in others may indeed be exaggerated and over the top. It may signal a lack of respect for appropriate boundaries. What is relevant here is my automatic mental response of "I'd *never* do that! I'm nothing like those individuals." Nevertheless, if we want to move beyond emotional stuckness, we must be starkly honest with ourselves. Rating our behavior against that of others, thinking ours is okay because it is not "that bad," will do little to advance our emotional health. We must be willing to look at where we possess seeds of the darker human behavior we rail against, so that we can reconcile our own darker impulses, harness the hidden gifts they offer, and integrate our warring selves.

By acknowledging my shadow qualities, I can short-circuit the inevitable buildup of psychic pressure that would surely have resulted had I suppressed my emotions and impulses. The emotional outlet that I give myself simply by admitting the truth of who I am and what I feel in totality acts as a safety valve for such pressure and reduces the likelihood that I will behave to the detriment of myself and others.

So would I ever stand at a salad bar and help myself to food in the way I observed someone else did? Well, if for some reason extreme circumstances led me to feel as though I needed to, what came up for me in that priceless moment at the workshop was that I surely wouldn't be as transparent as the woman and her husband. I would be much more discreet. Discreet . . . perhaps that's just a nicer way of saying covert, sneaky, slippery, for my guess is that I would hide my desperation better. I suppose I can add those qualities to my shadow list as well.

# CHAPTER 6

# Let There Be Dark

*"I am what I am."*
—Popeye, 1929

Self-acceptance, according to philosopher, sailorman, and comic book character from the 1920s, Popeye the Sailor, can best be summed up with his signature mantra, "I am what I am." Many in the field of psychiatry have long since agreed. The term self-acceptance is to be taken literally: acceptance of self. This does not mean selective acceptance or once-in-a-while acceptance, or I will accept only what I like about myself acceptance. It means to be in as full recognition as possible of who we are, including the messy parts. Most especially the messy parts, with no conditions. Central to acceptance is awareness. We cannot recognize what we cannot see; and if we're blind to certain personal truths, we are keeping ourselves in a state of relative unawareness.

Self-acceptance refers to a basic attitude toward oneself, an attitude of self-respect and self-validation. Not for being any particular way, good or bad, or achieving any specific goal, small or large, but for the willingness to see without censorship or punishment, the naked truth of who we are and what we have lived through.

It is important to note here that accepting ourselves for who we are does not mean that we approve of every part of our personality, nor does it mean that we give up on changing and growing. On the contrary, it is the starting point for change. The more we can let go of the push-pull within, the tug-of-war that comes from denying the truth of our real selves, the greater access we have to this truth. Our willingness to look honestly at our darker feelings and impulses is what gives them their proper release. Conscious recognition of suppressed feelings is a relief valve and an essential step for getting unstuck. When we allow this recognition to occur, mental blocks begin to dissolve, and our natural flow of energy can be restored. The disconnection that previously dominated our approach to living can be healed and the path to integration forged.

When it comes to looking at these darker truths, the reality is that most of us would rather not. We enjoy the comfort we feel just being us, even when this habit takes us down an unfulfilling road. The "us" that we are most comfortable with is the "us" we know. Or think we do.

Who and what we think we are informs how we navigate our world. This innermost vision influences all our significant life choices and decisions, ultimately shaping the kind of life we create. No aspect of our lives goes unaffected. Our deeply embedded self-concept determines everything, from the partner we choose, if we choose one at all, to the way we function in relationships, to what we tolerate in situations, to how we parent and govern, to the kinds of experiences we're drawn to, and ultimately how successful and fulfilled we are likely to be. Who we think we are has either supported or subverted our healthiest development.

This can be seen in the smallest and largest of ways. For instance, have you ever noticed the different ways in which people interpret or react to the same situation or event? I find this particularly interesting, especially when working with couples.

I am reminded of this small but illustrative example described by a couple I once saw for marital work. They were on a long-awaited vacation in the western portion of the United States. The Grand Canyon was to have been the highlight of their trip. When they arrived at the South Rim of the Canyon, they spent the better part of the first day making their way to one of the most popular viewpoints where visitors could peer one mile straight down into the heart of the Grand Canyon, the Colorado River. Filled with awe and almost moved to tears, one of the women marveled at the vastness and felt utterly humbled, inspired, and speechless, settling in to gaze for a longer period of time as she took in the breathtaking experience. Her partner, standing in the same spot experienced a wave of paralysis wash over her. Unable to speak (for an entirely different reason), she felt dwarfed, terrified, insignificant, and immediately wanted to escape, trying to stave off a panic attack. Two people, two completely different experiences. (It's not uncommon for these individuals to date or marry one another.) Whose reaction is more "appropriate?"

From an objective point of view, we might say the first person had a more fitting reaction to seeing the wonder that is the Grand Canyon, or certainly a more typical one. On the other hand, the second person, who became uncomfortable and panicky, was likely reacting to an internal cue, some sensory signal that told her standing in a vastly open space was unsafe, psychically. Phobias such as agoraphobia, a fear of open or public spaces, can have its roots in a variety of underlying causes. The point here is that this individual was not trying to be difficult or intentionally incompatible with her traveling partner. She was clearly reacting to her internal state, making her behavior seem irrational and illogical to the observing eye but probably very understandable in the context of her psychological history.

Here is another example, an exchange I observed recently while at a Broadway theater. Two people were about to take their seats moments before the curtain. Just as they settled into their respective places, two other ticket holders arrived and claimed the seats as their own. One of the persons already seated interpreted this as an irritating intrusion, got defensive, and mumbled something about calling security. The other assumed that the latecomers had made an innocent mistake and calmly suggested that each of them simply takes a second look at their tickets to clarify everyone's seat number. After an awkward interaction, it was apparent that it was the seated couple who had made the error. Embarrassed, they were ushered to their correct seats (which happened to be several rows closer to the stage).

In other words, the way we take in life's experiences is framed by who and what we think of ourselves and others and, in turn, helps to shape our world view. The sequence of "thought clicks," if you will, that pass through our mind in an instant determine how we handle virtually every situation that comes our way. That sequence is as follows: 1) Perception leads to thought, 2) Thoughts lead to feelings, 3) Feelings lead to behaviors.

While there are many variables that could inform how we react to our environment in any given moment such as mood, health, blood sugar, or the urgency of a situation, it is our core beliefs that most powerfully frame our perceptions.

Imagine someone who has felt taken advantage of in his early life. Conditioned to feel that he may be manipulated or used for someone else's gain, this individual might be on constant guard to protect himself from those whom he perceives as "takers." His reflex might be to root out such people wherever he goes. Given this, the more reactive individual in our theater example may have viewed the other ticket holders as precisely the type of predator he must guard against. On the other hand, if one has felt adequately supported in life, his/her basic outlook on others may lean toward benevolence and an underlying trust that things will work out in everyone's favor. We tend to expect more of what we have already experienced. We become what we have lived.

Our Grand Canyon scenario depicts individuals who have had distinctly different early life experiences. The individual who became terrified, it turns out, had a childhood in which the most basic and crucial boundary of physical safety was breached. She endured instances of physical abuse and humiliation. While this young woman in her thirties has a complex family history, it would not be difficult to understand how losing her mother suddenly at the age of nine and living with her overwhelmed and abusive father who drank excessively would be enough to predispose her to steep emotional and interpersonal challenges. Her difficulties illustrate some of the ways in which childhood feelings of unsafety, lack of adult protection, exposure to danger, feeling inadequately or poorly supported can and do manifest in seemingly strange ways.

The internalized experience of growing up emotionally unsupported and worse, harmed by the very person or persons whose job it was to provide protection, can easily turn a vulnerable child into an adult who is unable to withstand uncertainty of any kind and for whom the very ground underfoot is not to be trusted. For this individual, anything that sets off unconscious alarms that she is alone and unprotected triggers childhood terror, the root cause of which even she may be unaware. The Grand Canyon, while breathtakingly beautiful, also evoked deep feelings of insignificance and unsafety. The anxiety generated by this was simply too much for the young woman to bear. In her mind, the feeling of standing at the edge of an abyss activated similar childhood feelings in which she felt she was on the brink of a family disaster, utterly ungrounded and fundamentally unsafe. When the brain is faced with a situation that echoes a threatening childhood experience, decisive survival responses take over. In this case, the young woman took flight to her car, away from the literal and psychological "edge," to keep herself safe.

How you got to be you, and I got to be me, is a destination point along a fascinating journey that began without our conscious knowledge or consent. Our storyline was influenced by the key people in our lives who may have had little awareness of the personality they were shaping. The following is an example of exactly that. Notice how the authenticity of the children you're about to meet, particularly the daughter, is shaped— thwarted, really—by her parents' reactions and words.

\ ' / /

## CHAPTER 7

/ / , \ `

# Families

**M**ost of us are born into dysfunctional families.
Ask anyone with parents.

Not the alcoholic, abusive or neglectful kind necessarily, but more often the well-meaning and unaware ones. The parents who were anxious, conflicted, preoccupied, grieving, overwhelmed, immature, ill, or otherwise unable to see beyond their own emotional blind spots to adequately dole out what we needed and deserved. The ones who raised us scarcely better than they were raised and for whom bootstraps were the only means of getting up and out of difficult times. The ones who lacked the ability to acknowledge our feelings and respect our individuality. In other words, the average home.

To illustrate this further, imagine the following scene: (It is adapted from a conversation between two outstanding specialists in the fields of family therapy and self-esteem, Virginia Satir and Nathaniel Branden, as described in Nathaniel Branden's book, *Honoring the Self*, 1983.)

Parents and their two young children are sitting at the dinner table. The mother appears upset about something. The daughter, noticing the look of unhappiness on her mother's face asks, "What's the matter, Mommy?"

The mother replies in a tight, clipped tone of voice, "Nothing's the matter. I'm fine."

"But you are crying," insists the child, "Are you sad? Do you have a stomachache?" she continues, a hint of anxiety in her voice. The young girl recalled how she had a tummy ache recently that hurt so badly it made her cry.

The father now steps in and admonishes his wife for crying at the table and scolds the girl, saying, "You've upset your mother!"

The other child, older by two years, begins to laugh nervously, which upsets the dad even further. The girl begins to cry. The mother turns to her husband and says through her clenched teeth, "Now look at what you've done!"

The dad shouts angrily, "Hurry up and finish your dinner! Can't there ever be any peace in this house? I guess maybe when you damn kids are old enough to leave home!"

Tears stream down the mother's face.

The daughter looks at her parents with confusion and bewilderment. She feels hurt, scared, and utterly responsible for what just occurred. After pushing the food around on her plate, too upset to eat, she runs outside to play, a frantic effort to block out what just occurred.

Admittedly, it can be difficult to keep from wincing at this vignette, either because we simply feel for everyone involved or because something about that kitchen table reminds us of our own. Yet, it is only by looking further into this that we come to understand how "ordinary" occurrences such as parental dishonesty, invalidating, criticizing, blaming, and deflecting give rise to childhood escapism through defense mechanisms such as repression, blocking, avoidance, busying, fantasizing, internalization, and somatization.

We will see how these coping strategies, initially developed in childhood for emotional survival, later become the invisible bricks in our wall of self-protection. What started as a shield around our vulnerabilities ended up as a fortress around our hearts. The armor that was supposed to keep hurt out has somehow kept love from getting in. Along the way, we become estranged from our deepest selves and, in many cases, from the emotional closeness we so deeply crave. Since we can only allow others to get as close to us as we are to ourselves, this protective wall blocks our capacity to get close to others and sustain true emotional intimacy.

This can feel as confusing as it is disappointing. It can leave us with a self-perception that something is wrong with us, that we lack a certain competency with which to live life. What is really lacking is the awareness that we have lost a part of ourselves and the knowledge of how to get it back.

Were we to meet the child in our kitchen table scenario years later, we might encounter any of the adults described in this book—a person whose self-determination is hindered because she doesn't feel as though she is enough. Only by "unpacking" the family's conversation can we come to understand the hidden dynamics that will later serve as (problematic) guiding principles in the child's adult life.

By breaking down the conversation, line by line, certain key factors are revealed that shed light on the family members' inner workings. Firstly, the child perceives (accurately) that her mother is troubled by something. Mother reacts by invalidating her daughter's (correct) perception of reality. In effect, she lies. Perhaps she does so motivated by a misguided need to "protect" her child, or because she isn't sure how to comfort her. Or perhaps she doesn't know how to deal with her own unhappiness. Had she said something like, "Yes, sweetheart, Mommy is feeling a little sad right now but it's alright," she would have validated the child's accurate perception. By acknowledging her own truth (her unhappiness) simply and directly, without going into detail, she would have both received the child's compassion and reinforced it. The child would have been made to feel that a very natural part of her—her sensitivity—has value and meaning. An important lesson about empathy as well as giving and receiving could have been taught. Additionally, the notion of emotional pain could have been demystified rather than denied, which could have supported a healthier attitude toward it.

The father, perhaps to "protect" his wife from feeling vulnerable or perhaps out of guilt for not knowing how to comfort her himself, criticizes and scolds their daughter, thus adding to the incredulousness of the situation. If the mother is not sad, what is the harm in asking? If she is sad, why was the child made to feel wrong for guessing accurately what she was feeling? And why lie about it? To compound matters, mother yells at father, which further pushes the daughter into feeling guilty that she has set off a chain reaction of negative feelings among her family members.

How in the world is a child to perceive this situation?

As human beings, we are constantly striving to interpret our environment to make sense of things. We try to explain the unexplainable, lessen ambiguities, find certainty, and control our fate as much as possible. To this end, when we cannot sufficiently understand what is going on around us, we devise ways of bending reality to suit our interpretations and satisfy our need for safety and security. We make up or distort facts, fill in the blanks, deny the truth, or excuse it away. When all else fails, we try to escape by whatever means is necessary. For some adults, it is in the emotional blackout afforded us by alcohol or other substances. For others, it's under the fog of carbohydrates and sugar. For still others, numbing is found amidst excessive partying, drama, gossip, or busyness. There are countless ways in which the child in us frantically runs outside to play.

Like the young child at the family table, when faced with the incomprehensibility of a situation, we naturally try to normalize it for ourselves. Even if that means telling ourselves it's our fault that . . . Mommy is unhappy, or Daddy is angry, or things aren't getting any better. By accepting the blame that is placed on us or by assigning it to ourselves, we absorb the unrealistic burden of "fixing" things, thereby giving us the illusion of control. We develop a faulty belief that if we are the cause of the problem, we might also be its cure. If only we could figure out how. For many, figuring it out becomes a lifelong pursuit.

The responsibility we feel for causing our parents to be the imperfect caregivers they were is enormous. Believing that we have the power to change them into more satisfying parents has caused us to go through life with the relentless pursuit of a happier ending to our childhood story. By playing out childhood roles in adult relationships, mentally turning our partners into understudies for our flawed parents, we unconsciously set out to rewrite our history.

Here's what it looks like:

If one had a father who was emotionally unavailable, for example, there could be a strong unconscious pull toward other emotionally unavailable people in the hope of getting them to do what the unavailable parent could not: be emotionally present and provide unconditional love. The greater the resemblance to the disappointing parent (not necessarily in conspicuous ways, but on more subtle levels), the sweeter the satisfaction of unlocking the gems we believe exist in the parental substitute. Many people end up with romantic partners curiously like the parent with whom they had the greater difficulty. We are unconsciously compelled to give ourselves better endings to our past. Those who are more emotionally available may not seem as attractive to the individual who was raised with emotional distance, because the "chemistry" that includes the excitement of finally winning over the person is not present. Like a fish out of water, there is nothing to strive for, nothing to prove, no one to "convince" to love us if another's interest is forthcoming. As a result, the emotionally available person can seem boring or dull. Absent the tension of conquering the emotionally remote person, the chemistry can feel flat. Having our emotional needs met by someone who is enough like the parent who let us down holds the promise of a dream come true. Unfortunately however, this dream too often leads to nightmarish disappointment.

This has led many of us to lose ourselves in the hope of finding the hidden treasure in the people we select, to find emotion in the emotionally cut off, thoughtful consideration in the self-absorbed, and sober reasoning in the addicted. Our fantasy is that when we do (if only we could), we will finally have the love we have longed for all our lives. Letting go of this hope is one of the most frightening things one can do, and therefore one of the most fought against. In our desperate desire to finally be loved the way we yearn to be loved, we cling to this hope at almost all costs, waiting and waiting for our time to come. We must begin to understand that, while we are waiting, we keep ourselves stuck.

Our lives are lived in relation to our family history. The ways in which we have dealt with the pain and shame of our own kitchen table scenarios, or rather how we escaped them, became much more than simply how we got through those specific times. Gradually, the coping strategy took on a broader meaning, woven into the fiber of our being. Those ways in which we ran outside to play (forget, block, repress, pretend, stay moving, take care of others, laugh things off, fantasize) seeped into our very way of being.

Absorbed into our core personality, these tactics did not merely ease a one-time event. They were the organizing coping strategies around which our character was formed and became part of a psychological blueprint designed to help us survive repeated disappointment, loneliness, unsafety, harshness, and feeling invisible.

Like the color of our eyes, these tactics became the part of our emotional makeup that we cannot see unless we look in the mirror. And the "mirror" happens to be whatever in life reflects the gap between who we are and who we pretend to be to feel loved. When we want one thing in life but keep getting another, this is a "mirror" experience—valuable information that shows us where we can look more deeply into the patterns we run and the pain we hide. There is no coming unstuck in our lives until we process this information.

## CHAPTER 8

# Walls, Shields, and Cover-Ups

As is clear now, when events and conflicts in our lives cause emotional pain, we frequently develop unconscious attitudes and ways of behaving to protect us from distress. These specific strategies, known as defense mechanisms, make and keep us unaware of impulses, feelings, and memories that are unacceptable to our conscious mind and our overall view of ourselves.

Defense mechanisms exist exclusively to help us maintain emotional comfort and safety. They serve as gatekeepers to that part of the psyche where our most painful feelings, memories, and impulses reside, keeping out and covering up any unwanted ones that would threaten our emotional stability. Although they mask our deepest emotions, this does not mean the emotions are silenced; they find ways of making themselves known nonetheless.

Note how the cycle of emotional release and emotional suppression plays out: First, an uncomfortable or painful event occurs, then the emotion generated by that event produces an impulse in you. The event, emotion, and resulting impulse are all charged with a certain degree of distress, pain, and "energy." (Energy refers to the emergence of bodily sensations that are produced by a thought.) Butterflies in the stomach, the exciting thought of a new love, a sinking feeling in your belly at the thought of receiving sad news, perspiration at the thought of getting rejected are examples of the link between thought, emotion, and physical sensation.

As an impulse arises such as anger, it is accompanied by a fantasied or imagined action, often an unconscious one, such as lashing out in some way, even physically. We may have the urge to yell, shake, or hit the person we are angry with. Because most of us see ourselves as nonviolent, the thought of lashing out feels out of sync with who we are. The thought of lashing out can also produce fears of negative consequences such as punishment or retaliation. Sensing the "unacceptable" nature of such an impulse, our unconscious mind automatically engages one or more defense mechanisms to suppress the angry or aggressive outburst, thereby keeping a tight lid on our impulses. This works effectively to keep us from lashing out at one another, and that is a good thing. At the same time however, it can leave us with a deep sense that our emotions are bad, wrong, dangerous, or something to feel ashamed of. Our unconscious solution is: don't be that, don't do that, don't show that, and/or don't feel that. Over time, this can amount to an internal experience of not being on friendly terms with ourselves, leading to all sorts of problems moving forward. Our young gymnast was right.

## A Word About Emotions Themselves

We are not always tuned into exactly what triggers our emotions. We might think of them as mysterious "mood waves" that originate out of the blue, leaving us awash in a perplexing, invisible goo. Often we have no idea how the gooey waves arrived or what to do to get them to leave. Worse, their onset can seem not only random but unsubstantiated, and we can feel as though we are helplessly at their mercy. Science has different ways of explaining emotions, but the consensus among scientists is that emotions are anything but random. Unless we learn to decode the information provided by emotions and harness the power of this information, we remain at a loss for how to steer our lives toward the satisfaction we want, stuck in a feedback loop of constantly hiding from what we feel.

Awareness of our emotions is key to everything we desire. Why? Because we are constantly responding to cues all around and within us whether we realize it or not. We interpret these cues through our physical senses and interpret them as good or bad, safe or dangerous, painful or pleasurable. Emotions are the evidence that reflects to us how we respond to our environment: with fear, anger, joy, sadness. We identify these emotional reactions via the sensations in our body, known as feelings. This phenomenon, the ability to make conscious contact with these feelings (the tangible, physical concomitants of emotions), is at the heart of healthy emotional functioning.

Learning something about how our brain, body, and mind communicate with one another is essential for understanding where emotions come from and how they are released. If not permitted their proper expression, suppressed emotions will result in problems of all types, including compromised mental health and physical ailments of various kinds. To be unaware of the powerful operating system that runs much of our decision making is to remain disconnected from the neurobiological engine that drives us either closer or farther away from a happier and more harmonious life.

## Releasing Emotions

Emotions have a natural way of being released. When triggered by a thought such as, *This outcome isn't fair*, or *If I start crying, I'll never stop*, or *I'll never get ahead*, or *I'm afraid to be alone*, the brain and nervous system govern an upward flow of bodily sensations associated with these thoughts. These sensations are experienced in and throughout the entire body. As mentioned, this explains why we cry when we're sad, get flushed when we're angry, smile when we're happy, and perspire when we're anxious. When suppressed however, the energy (upward surge) behind our emotions can literally get stuck in the body, manifesting as a variety of physical symptoms. Everything from stiff shoulders to migraines to high blood pressure to weight gain among countless other symptoms can result when the natural flow of emotional energy is blocked. How then are these trapped emotions released?

To begin with, there is a huge difference between experiencing an emotion and mentally comprehending or labeling it. Saying, "I know I am angry," is one thing. Being able to face and experience it is quite another. Note that when I say "face the feeling," I am not talking about acting it out. Instead, I am referring to the ability to identify the emotion, experience it in the body in the present moment as a feeling, and link it to the specific event or memory from which it originated. If working with a practitioner, this is carried out in the safety and confidentiality of the practitioner's care, either in person or remotely (using a secure technology platform.)

When the memory or event is recalled and focused upon, the amygdala (stress center) and the limbic system (emotional center) in the brain are engaged. The feelings in the body are "live," so to speak. Otherwise, if the emotion is simply described, recounted, or narrated, it will not be accessible. While many healing modalities work with feelings in different ways, the "embodied approaches" work best to get at the emotions that are stuck in the body. As such, it is only by allowing the experience to come to life that it can truly be released and the energy behind it neutralized. In a following chapter, we will see how one such approach, Emotional Freedom Techniques (EFT), known as "tapping," combines embodied methods with cognitive ones to facilitate the release of suppressed emotions. By utilizing gentle and subtle EFT interventions, for example, "the movie technique," in which the troubling issue is approached as though you are watching it on a screen at a safe distance, you can begin to desensitize yourself from highly charged emotions. You can easily learn the basics of EFT in a later chapter.

Desensitization is the gradual reduction of the heightened reaction you have over a specific trigger such as an event, a memory, a physical sensation, or an object. Gradual exposure to the trigger simply by imagining it in an incremental and systematic way, and coupling it with meridian tapping, calms the revved-up activity in the brain. The brain's anxious, arousal reflex is replaced with a relaxation response. You can literally begin to lessen your sensitivity to a disturbing emotional trigger.

As the veil of anxiety is lifted, emotions and the memories that produced them can be seen more directly. From this perspective, the darker components of shame, self-judgment, and guilt that have plagued your life may be reviewed and re-evaluated. With a clearer, more adult view of past events and circumstances, the opportunity exists for you to understand your childhood reactions within a broader and more realistic context. Instead of clinging to a binary, black-or-white, all-or nothing, good-or-bad way of seeing yourself, a child's view, you can better grasp the complexities of your early life and the people in it. Your emotional mindset expands from that of a one-dimensional child to a more multidimensional adult.

As painful and upsetting emotions are worked through (I prefer to use the term "metabolized," which connotes di-gesting, utilizing what serves you, eliminating what doesn't), you come to recognize the profound impact that unacknowl-edged feelings and their defenses have had on your life: your relationships, your mental and physical health, your success and happiness. The more you face the fact that much of your effort over the course of your life has been misguided, i.e., you've been looking feverishly for that sunrise in the west, the more you will realize that you have missed opportunities and have lost time that you cannot get back. This may bring about some sadness and even depressive feelings. Do not lose heart. This is legitimate grieving and is a natural, and neces-sary part of the working-through process. As such, it should not be avoided. More importantly, it can serve as a deep and abiding reminder that you have future opportunities in which to choose differently and more wisely.

## Defense Mechanisms

Most people tend to handle their emotions as they were taught (or forced) to do in childhood, taking their cues from their parents or caretakers. Whether modeled directly by the adults in our lives who may have never talked about their feelings, or forced to deal with unpleasant, painful, confusing, or harmful family dynamics by inventing ways of coping with them, defense mechanisms are the unconscious "super powers" that we developed as children to keep ourselves safe. There are different types and we will take a brief look at the most common ones now.

People do not utilize just one defense. Typically, we use several in conjunction with one another. In his book, *Think Like a Shrink* (1992), Christ Zois, MD, discusses defenses in detail. A noted authority in the field of short-term dynamic psychotherapy, Dr. Zois was instrumental in the advancement of an accelerated treatment method in which sessions were video recorded for in-depth study, ensuring that the treatment was both brief and effective, quite an innovative development at the time. By micro-analyzing the recordings, he was able to pinpoint the uses as well as the working through of defense mechanisms with remarkable depth and understanding.

I had the opportunity to attend several of Dr. Zois's lectures early in my clinical training and observed his recordings personally along with a small group of colleagues in New York. The following is a modified explanation of his description of defense mechanisms elucidated in his work. This fascinating information sheds crucial light on how we humans manage to turn against ourselves even as we seek to do just the opposite.

# The Three Types of Defenses

Defenses fall into three categories. While we tend to rely on one category over another, attitudes and behavior from all three often overlap in our personalities.

*Vagueness.* Relying on nonspecific thoughts and feelings, passivity, and adopting a victim stance are all attempts to escape the pain of an event, an unpleasant memory, or the urge to act in a negative way.

We commonly use vagueness to avoid making a commitment to a specific thought or feeling. People who use vagueness qualify important statements with such words and phrases as "I think," "probably," "maybe," "I'm not sure," and "sometimes." In a further effort to keep from being focused and specific, they tend to generalize and use language such as "everybody," "all the time," and "never."

It is not unusual that individuals who utilize this defense tend to be ambivalent when it comes to important issues in their lives. Being vague and nonspecific inhibits clarity of thought and keeps you from focusing on what is really bothering you.

*Passivity and Helplessness.* Adopting a passive position is one way to avoid taking action, getting on with an issue, or moving forward with your life. Frequently uttered statements such as "I don't make enough money in my present job, but I don't know what else to do," "I don't know what to do to help myself," or "I just can't make a decision," indicate signs of feeling helpless. While it is appropriate to consult with others from time to time, and it is certainly constructive to ask for help, a general approach to life in which one says "I can't," "I don't know how," or "What should I do?" signals a type of stubbornness or even an underlying refusal to take care of oneself. It is a posture that wraps "I won't" in "I can't."

Passivity is not laziness. It is used to mask emotions, both past and current, particularly intense anger or deep pain or hurt. The fear of expressing anger or a grievance can be so great that doing nothing, regardless of how self-defeating, is preferable. The underlying pain and hurt can be so intense that inertia appears to be a better choice than facing the problem. Such a pattern of holding in anger or pain from the past will almost certainly cause the same anger or pain to be injected into the future, where it will become more ingrained, not less.

## The Emotional Defenses

Emotional defenses are emotions that are used to mask underlying pain. Although the individual experiences the defending emotion, it is not the deepest emotion. The defending emotion is used as a cover for the deeper and more threatening one. The most common emotional defenses are weepiness, depression, and anger.

*Weepiness*. A common defense, weepiness is often used to hide deep anger and sometimes to mask pain and guilt. A father takes away the iPad from his son as a punishment for instance, and the boy bursts into tears; he is not sad or hurt. He is enraged at his father. Or a woman says of her boss, "Whenever she (the boss) criticizes me, I start to cry." This is not sadness. What she genuinely wants to do is tell off her boss.

You are not always crying because you feel sad. Sometimes people say, "I got so angry I broke down in tears. But such crying is not an expression of anger. Rather it is a cover for it. Similarly, responding with tears to frustration, guilt, or anger is a way of avoiding these underlying emotions.

If you find yourself in tears, ask yourself if you are crying because of sadness or grief, or if you are reacting to a situation that is out of your control. The frustration that you may be feeling could likely bring about a deeper feeling of anger that you would rather not feel. It is safer to melt into a puddle of tears rather than admit the deeper truth that you are angry. Your relationship to the person with whom you may feel angry plays a factor as well. Feeling angry toward an authority figure can be threatening, especially if one worries about retaliation. Likewise, uncovering longstanding anger toward a parent or parental figure who is now aged, infirmed, dying, or deceased can arouse feelings of guilt to the point where cutting off the deeper anger seems preferable.

***Depression.*** Anger can be so intense and threatening that it is difficult to tolerate and, as a defense, you become depressed. The depression becomes a means of not dealing with angry emotions, because if you are overwhelmed by depression you are immobilized and thus incapable of lashing out. Again I am emphasizing the point that literally lashing out toward another living being is never an appropriate or wise option. I am saying that as long as we *depress* the recognition of the anger, we keep ourselves from knowing how to respond to it in a constructive way. When we acknowledge our anger for what it is, we can take specific steps to mitigate it, such as reestablishing a boundary, saying "no," or asking for help. When we defend against conscious admission of our anger by going to depression, the heaviness and depletion that is experienced ensures that the hidden anger will not escape. Anger is internalized and thus turned in on the self. In effect, it is easier to be angrier at yourself than toward someone whom you need, love, or are accountable to.

Defensive depression differs from authentic depression. Authentic depression results from a significant loss: the death of a loved one, the loss of a job, lifestyle, an unresolved circumstance, health concerns, and many other anguishing or crushing situations. In those instances, it is natural and normal to feel sad and bereft. The grieving process is necessary and healthy.

One important distinction between grief and defensive depression is that the defensive type almost always involves a sense of self-evaluation. With grief, there is an actual loss, and it is expected that following an undefined period of mourning, the loss will be integrated and lived with, albeit with some residual sadness.

With defensive depression, the sufferer almost always feels badly about the self, evaluating, or more to the point, devaluing the self. "She left me because I wasn't good enough to keep her." "I lost the pregnancy because I don't deserve to be happy." The depressing event also involves a loss but is interpreted as a type of rejection which compounds the individual's already negative self-view.

It is sometimes difficult for someone who is depressed to differentiate between the types of depression, and therefore a consultation with a professional is warranted. Note that there are other kinds of depression that do not fall into either category of grief or defensive depression. For a variety of reasons, including genetic predisposition, some sufferers of severe depression may require medication and sometimes hospitalization. While there are cases in which therapy and medication work successfully together, such examples are beyond the scope of this book.

*Anger.* Just as depression can be used as a defense against anger, anger can be used as a defense against deeper feelings of vulnerability, pain, and sorrow. There are two kinds of anger. One is an appropriate response to an attack, threat, or injustice, and the other derives from a deeper sense of hurt, insecurity, inadequacy, or inferiority. Because anger is a more energetically charged emotion, it is frequently used as a mask for powerlessness and helplessness. For many, it is easier to feel artificially pumped up and worked up about something than it is to feel deflated or hopeless.

I treat many people who walk around with a hair-trigger temperament. They are easily activated or set off as they react to the slightest provocation (or no provocation at all). Underneath their rage lies enormous pain. Regardless of how draining it is for them to feel chronically angry and endure the interpersonal consequences of their angry demeanor, they find it easier to pay that price than to feel their emotional pain.

## The Intellectual Defenses

On the other side of the defense mechanism coin are the defenses that utilize the cognitive aspects of the psyche—the intellect. While the emotional defenses that were just described can be tricky to unravel because they substitute one emotion for another deeper one, the intellectual defenses avoid emotions altogether. Users of this type of defense mechanism tend to layer justifications, excuses, and jargon to explain their behavior and patterns. Their "arguments" for their positions tend to be airtight and difficult to penetrate. Effective strategies for keeping unwanted emotions from coming into consciousness, intellectual defenses seem objective and credible. Nevertheless, when used excessively, they prevent authentic emotions from being faced and processed.

Among the most-used intellectual defenses are rationalization, intellectualization, avoidance, denial, and projection. A brief definition of each one follows.

*Rationalization.* Perhaps the most used of the intellectual defenses, rationalization means what it says: you provide reasons to justify your attitudes and behavior and those of others.

Question: "What was it like when your boss suddenly fired you?"

Response: "Well, what else could he do? His boss was pressuring him to cut costs."

Containing a kernel of truth (the boss was being pressured), the rationalized response focuses exclusively on the validity of the situation but excludes any contact with the emotion. In effect, the emotional impact is virtually denied. The biggest problem with this defense is that its users believe their rationalizations. If one wishes to be totally honest with oneself, the justifications must be put aside, and the hard and messy underlying issues (guilt, fear, shame) must be dealt with.

*Intellectualization.* Intellectualization is going into philosophical and lofty ideals as a way of moving away from what is truly bothering you. Unlike rationalization, which involves specific reasons and excuses for your behavior, intellectualization retreats into the general, nonspecific way of looking at a situation.

People who intellectualize do not usually talk about themselves or the issue they are dealing with directly or personally. Intellectualization is geared toward inaction: "What can you do?" or "This sort of thing happens all the time," or "It's just my turn at misery, that's all." Thoughts, even if intellectually valid, are used in the service of distancing from feelings. Impersonal and abstract, they seldom make people feel better because the deeper issues are left untouched.

*Avoidance.* Avoidance takes different forms and when used as a defense mechanism, it involves the practice of staying away from situations that are emotionally stirring. Avoidance is typically used when faced with overwhelming feelings such as anger. Often people confuse the avoidance of an emotion with the emotion itself: "I got so angry with him, I stormed out of the room." Such a statement does not express what you felt and how you experienced it; it explains what you did in *response* to what you felt. Avoidance is a tactic to steer yourself away from just how angry or hurt you are.

Some use this defense in a broader way, avoiding other people. They decline invitations and tend not to seek out other people. This mechanism is a vehicle for defending against intimacy and keeps one invisible to a certain extent.

*Denial.* Denial is a tricky defense mechanism that can take place on various levels of the psyche. Denial is used to distort either the reality of an external situation ("I drew the largest crowd in history") or an internal state ("I know I've been charged with two DUIs, but I don't have a drinking problem. The system is just out for me!") so that one can live a relatively disturbance-free existence.

People who use denial are often at odds with others' assessments of them and they are not particularly receptive to feedback.

Because individuals who rely on this defense isolate thought from emotion, their denial may be due to their unawareness that feelings exist. Others use it when they are confronted with a painful truth and are otherwise unable to explain it away. These individuals do not face the real issues that are bothering them.

*Projection.* When we sense on a deep level that there is something about ourselves that we do not want to own or acknowledge, we might project or "toss" the unwelcomed trait, characteristic, or behavior onto someone else. The distinguishing feature of projection is the pattern of attributing our unacceptable qualities to another person, seeing in them what we are blind to in ourselves. Especially relevant to the theme of this book, projection is the primary way in which we ignore unwanted aspects of ourselves out of a fearful belief that they make us undesirable or unlovable.

*Displacement.* Displacement is the shifting of an impulse, usually aggression, away from the cause and onto a powerless substitute. For example, a man is enraged at his father for being self-absorbed, critical, and dismissive but cannot confront him directly for fear of retaliation or some other severe consequence such as being pushed away or cut off. What he does instead is "transfer" his intense anger onto someone who is less likely to push back. That person could be a spouse or a child, someone who will absorb the "attack" that is really meant for the father. It is easier and safer to direct one's anger toward a less powerful person rather than toward the target person.

*Compartmentalization.* Compartmentalization is the unconscious process of isolating conflicting thoughts and feelings and mentally "placing" them in separate "compartments" that do not overlap. An example of this is a person who had a serious, upsetting argument with her spouse in the morning, but places her feelings toward her husband in a mental "box" to deliver an important presentation at work. This is a commonly used defense mechanism and (in this instance) is utilized appropriately to check her personal life at the door. An example of a more fragmented personality style is a greedy businessman who spends his work week low-balling, undercutting, manipulating, conning, and doing all he can to acquire material gain for his company only to attend church on Sunday where he listens to homilies that emphasize brotherhood, sisterhood, and generosity. He sincerely believes he is following the spiritual teachings of his church, completely unaware that he lives in a manner contradictory to his beliefs.

## Is It Ever Helpful to Use Defenses?

Defense mechanisms are natural and normal. No one can go through life completely exposed and vulnerable to unending internal and external threats to our emotional safety and comfort. It is when the use of our defenses runs us rather than the other way around that they become problematic.

# How To Detect When You're Being Overly Defensive

While defenses are natural, their overuse creates difficulties. Self-monitoring is the best way to discern whether your use of defenses is excessive and therefore counterproductive. Such overuse suggests you are likely avoiding deeper issues in your life. An indication of this is when you notice yourself justifying your actions or rationalizing your unhappiness, having little to show for it except lost time and missed opportunities. Although a painful realization, this is information reflecting itself to you so that you can consider other ways of dealing with things in your life. The regret and grief that may surface as you begin to understand exactly how you have run from yourself is a valuable motivator and catalyst for change. You will need this reminder when you slip back into old patterns. It will act like a truthful friend. Try not to push this information away. Know that deflecting your pain by relying on defenses is not the only way to deal with hurt, emptiness, disappointment, and fear. Neither is swallowing your pain day after day, year after year. You can prevent this by gradually learning to admit what you have avoided so that you can be real with yourself, handle your emotion constructively, and in time be the wholly functioning adult that you were meant to be.

## Masquerading

These mechanisms serve to distance us from certain needs, feelings, fears, and longings, as we have seen. The lifelong, unconscious practice of denying our inner experience began in childhood. Undoing the consequences of this practice requires us to *access the engine* that drives the denial now, in our current lives.

In the unconscious, there are no clocks and no calendars. The future and the past are abstract concepts. Everything that runs in the unconscious mind is happening now. Like family videos recorded long ago and replayed for current viewing, the enactments seem to be reoccurring now. Whatever we lived through that has been repressed is buried alive. Just like the home movie, the memories, and emotions replay in the present. Until we allow ourselves to become unblocked and face what we have turned a blind eye to, we will continue to ignore the movie that runs within us. It is not surprising. Very few of us were taught how to deal with those old emotional scenes. We will continue to invalidate our own needs and remain terrified to face and experience the emotions that are an intimate part of us. We will be forever stuck in a sort of limbo between the person we are and the person we're telling ourselves we are. Seeing the truth of what lies beneath our facades cannot happen until the layers of defenses are penetrated.

How to best go about this has been debated by those in the psychiatric and related fields for many decades. In my experience, the most rapid and effective way to accomplish this unmasking is by applying Emotional Freedom Techniques (EFT) to unconscious emotional blocks and traumas. As we will see, this method is an exciting and elegant way for both client and practitioner to identify defenses and bring to light previously denied emotions and memories. Only when they are brought out into the open can they be released and ultimately integrated.

## What Happens When Masks and Facades Are Lifted?

Defenses are meant to protect, but like an overly vigilant parent with good intentions, this protection can over shield a child's ability to become independent. Rather than learn how to adapt to emotional challenges and balance one's feelings, the overly protected child is deprived of the resourcefulness with which to deal with life's most challenging circumstances securely and effectively. This leaves a child too often feeling like, well, . . . a child in adulthood.

To gain mastery over your defenses and feel confident enough to navigate the shifting and demanding emotional currents of life, you must first be willing to do a few things:

1. Take responsibility for living as an autonomous person, one who is connected to others but at the same time one who can stand apart from others.
2. See yourself on equal ground with others.
3. Develop the flexibility to maintain a core identity while at the same time be open to seeing things in new and expanding ways.
4. Be willing to go through the pain of awakening from the deep sleep of denial.

Dr. Christ Zois goes on to say in his work, "The transition from childhood to adulthood is sometimes painful, and so is the transition from a life that is encumbered by defenses to one that is free of them. To make that transition, you must suffer the pain of dealing with the real feelings you've been burying." I often tell my clients that waking up from denial is no easy task. Nor is it a feel-good undertaking. At least not at first. Emerging from a consciousness which has been numbed will bring previously avoided emotions to the surface. If the thought of this is making you uncomfortable, fear not. When utilizing a technique such as EFT and doing so with a skilled practitioner, the process is gradual, systematic, gentle, and, most important, safe.

The reward of shedding overused defenses is liberating. Once you have modified or reduced them, you can face the troubling feelings that have remained hidden beneath them. "Such confrontations which are more difficult in the antici-pation than in the doing, provide for emotional honesty and clarity, and they allow you to achieve intimacy and productive relationships with those around you." (*Think like a Shrink*, 1992). Finally, by allowing yourself to engage openly and honestly with yourself and others, you become exponentially better at being a full participant in your life. The need to hide behind tightly worn psychological masks will be lessened. You will still maintain your defenses; however, you will be more in control of them instead of being controlled by them.

In the section to follow, we will begin to demystify how our defensive masks work and look at a few of the most com-monly worn ones. I will describe the masks and cover-ups that many of my clients have adopted, what they look like, and how others may react to them. Perhaps you will recog-nize one or more of your own masks here.

## Decoding Masks

The best way for me to illustrate psychological masks and how they work is to give you a glimpse into one of mine (I have several). For the purposes of this book, I am going to put a spotlight on one of my most stubborn masks. Its creation involves ice cream, a beauty contest, and my father's appetite for perfectionism.

## There she is...

When I was a young girl between the ages of about eight and eleven, my father and I watched beauty pageants on television. We loved to settle in for this annual two-hour event with heaping bowls of pistachio ice cream and follow the fifty-one beautiful contestants all the way to the winner.

As I watched, I studied the hair, teeth, and posture of each contestant with the scrutiny of a forensic investigator. *How did these girls do it*? I wondered. *How did they prepare for this night? Are they always this beautiful? Do they even eat ice cream? And what about the end, when all the girls hug the winner? Do they mean it? Do they cry afterward?* I took this all very seriously.

So did my father. I remember the way he called out the pluses and minuses of each contestant, the way I imagined other dads watched sporting events. "She has beautiful hair! She has great skin. She's pretty, but not as pretty as the others." (If you're getting triggered by his sexism, hold on, we'll tap on that later.)

I catalogued each comment he made, and watched with some mixture of envy and competitiveness the detailed attention he paid to each girl's appearance.

I spent a lot of time pondering deeply what it took to become Miss America. Obviously, looking back, I was really pondering was what it took to capture my father's delight.

I thought and thought about those beautiful girls and secretly lamented how different we were from each other, Miss

Montana, and me. Still a vague dream that maybe one day I could be . . .

Well I don't know how or why, but for some reason Dad and I had an uncanny knack for picking the winner. I'd estimate our track record was around 90 percent. If, by some stroke of bad luck, "our girl" turned out to be a runner-up instead, we both shouted at the television. "C'mon! She got ripped off!," we'd bark. "Are you blind? Not fair!" Then we talked about it for days.

I assume my dad didn't give the whole thing much thought beyond that. I, on the other hand, still harken back to those evenings in our 1960's garden apartment living room. I think about how the likelihood of becoming a beauty queen was the gauge by which my self-esteem rose and fell. For my father, it turned out to be a not so well-hidden standard. The words "You'll never be Miss America" became a frequent refrain to most of the things I did that went awry.

"You've ruined your hair," is what he told me when I got a bad perm (too frizzy) a few days before starting ninth grade: "You'll never be Miss America." When I scraped my knee badly that year while going for a layup in basketball, he said, "Well now, with that terrible scar, you'll never be Miss America." When I chipped my front tooth drinking Coca-Cola from a glass bottle (our family pet, a toy poodle named Gigi, picked that exact moment to jump in my lap), and watched, stunned, as the humongous tooth fragment floated in the soda, I anticipated the disappointment in his voice and the words, "You've ruined your smile. You'll never be Miss America." And my personal favorite, "Did you ever notice that your eyes are a little too close together? You'll never . . .

You get the point.

Obviously I didn't become Miss America. Or Miss Hasbrouck Heights, New Jersey. The fact of the matter was, with that big scar on my knee and the bigger one on my self-esteem, I didn't even fully get to be Miss Catherine Duca. I was more of a runner-up in my own life.

The belief that I developed, catalyzed by those sweet evenings with my father where I witnessed both his appreciation of physical beauty and his propensity for criticism, cemented by what was clearly a breach of the Top Ten things never to say to a pre-adolescent daughter, was that I was not pretty enough to win his praise. I was too short and too scarred, too frizzy, and too flawed. There was simply nothing I could do to compare to what I thought was his ideal. From then on, I walked around as if everywhere I went, he and an internalized panel of judges trailed me.

At some point, I can't remember exactly when, I figured out that I could sometimes dodge them at the Lancôme counter, my secret a little safer there, beneath all those pretty lip glosses, eye shadows, and sleight-of-hand blush techniques.

Do you have anything to make my eyes look greener?" I once asked.

"No," said the supermodel/cosmetician in a whisper. ". . . but I might be able to make them look bigger and a little further apart." She got me. And so my obsession with makeup began. Make up for this inadequacy. Make up for that flaw. Make up for how demoralized I felt not being one of "them."

Now I love my dad. Before he died in my late thirties, I watched him overcome many hurdles in both his personal and business life. An interesting and complex mix of qualities, there was almost no one's company I enjoyed more. I loved listening to his stories, and he loved listening to mine.

He was funny, self-deprecating, and had tremendous empathy for others. He was always interested in whatever I was doing, eager to lend a hand, and without fail supported me in virtually every endeavor that mattered to me. He was my go-to person, always. A handsome looking man with the sparkliest eyes and prominent Roman nose, he made frequent sacrifices for those he loved. His generosity moves me to tears still. He was loving and kind and frequently went out of his way for strangers, just as he had for his family.

When I went through a fear-of-swallowing phase, for instance, after nearly choking on a Good 'n Plenty in the first grade, he sat up with me an entire night gently coaxing me with humor and silly jokes to take a baby aspirin. We played the 1, 2, 3 game where he and I would pop the aspirin in our mouths at the same time and swallow on the count of 3. Score: Dad, 3. Me, 0.

I remember that nothing worked, and my fever got worse. Finally, as the sun came up and peaked through the blinds making those sun stripes on our red Formica kitchen table, he had me visualize my throat as a giant waterfall and said the pill was just like a tiny pebble going over the edge. I could hardly stop laughing. Down the hatch it went! I went back to bed, my fever breaking just as my mother, a nurse who worked the night shift, came home, and took over. I know he went to work that day and probably many others without a single minute of sleep, and never once complained about it or made me feel guilty. I loved how nurturing he was.

He was always so thoughtful of others. There was the Christmas Eve he drove over two hours on slick roads to do a small job for an elderly customer who called in a panic about last-minute holiday guests. When he finished installing the new tile floor in her tiny kitchen, likely spending more on gas than he made in profit, she tipped him with two of the silver dollars that hung on her tree as ornaments. He held on to them ever since and said they reminded him of her generosity and appreciation. It must have made him feel good because he carried them in his pocket until the day he died, the markings completely rubbed off from the thirty years of jingling that I miss so much. No one made me feel as safe and loved as he did.

But there was his Miss America side, after all. Did I forget to mention that no one could slice and dice my self-confidence as sharply as him? In his effort to guide me, his Ginsu-like tactics could often inflame me, sometimes hurt me, and ultimately teach me to see myself as someone with potential, "if only."

Whether he intended it or not, and I doubt that he did, my self-image coalesced around some of the qualities he admired, but which I didn't possess. My personal view of myself was something like an algebraic equation where the "x" remained an unknown variable. Something was missing in me.

Though he never stated it, his Miss America references instilled in me a subtle sense that had I longer legs, greener eyes (my eyes are brown, by the way), no visible scars, and a Texan accent (or was that no accent? All I know is that I hate the accent I have), I might make it to good enough. If only I were different somehow, if only I were more.

John Duca was my hero, best friend, and crazy-making father, all blended into one paternal smoothie. The more I came to see him through the eyes of an adult, the more I understood his insecurities and appreciated his good, if sometimes misplaced, intentions. I recognized that his efforts to love and protect me were from the perspective of someone who was himself hurt and criticized.

Like so many of his generation, he had been down some difficult roads. His ethnicity was often disparaged, and he was ridiculed for his Roman nose, twice broken by neighborhood bullies. His muscular but smallish stature was the brunt of many jokes growing up. I was able to see that part of how he loved me was wanting to protect me from some of the pain he went through. I believe that he thought criticism from him would harden me to the criticism from others. "Nope, Dad, it didn't. But thanks for trying."

Coming to better understand my father as a person in his own right, with his unique history, fears, and facades has made it easier to accept my own all these years later. My panel of beauty pageant judges is more muffled now, although its echo is sometimes just a slip-up away. Nothing fires up my inner Miss Inadequacy faster than thinking I have done a less perfect job than I expect of myself. When this happens, it becomes another opportunity to work on one of the primary ways in which I stay stuck: trying to be flawless.

## My Mask of Perfectionist

Driven to hide how unbeautiful I felt, I decided to try to get my father's attention some other way, by doing things well. And by "well" I mean beyond his criticism. A daunting task (you know, you've met him), I suppose I was spurred on by the slim odds at achieving such a thing. The further the goal post, the harder I tried. Something deep within told me that winning my father's praise, no matter the longshot, would make all my striving worth the effort.

The voice in my head told me I could always do better. Not in the encouraging, melodic voice of a kind and gentle kindergarten teacher, but more in the spittle-laden bark of a drill sergeant hollering directly into my rough recruit ear: "Who do you think you are, you little chicken liver? Subtext: Miss America would n-e-e-ver do that! And if she did, she'd at least be twirling that god-forsaken baton. "What's wrong with you? You're going out dressed like that? (Read: you frizzy, scared, chipped-tooth, eyes-too-close together, you!) such was the noise that looped in my mind, 24/7.

And thus began my relentless pursuit of perfection, twisting my personality's DNA into a double helix of people-pleaser and over-thinker. Maintaining a facade free of cracks was the best way I could think of to win my dad's admiration. Like egg whites folded into a souffle, the quest for his approval was indistinguishable from what I thought of myself. The stress and frustration from striving to earn his approval tried to get my attention through frequent migraines and insomnia. I wish I had listened.

Somewhere along the line, I decided I would try letting all this go. I told myself that I simply wouldn't care so much about what he and others thought of me. Guess what? My mind wouldn't have any of that. I felt as if I was walking a tight rope, telling myself it didn't matter if I fell. My mind would not let me believe the bill of goods I was selling myself. Mr. Drill Sergeant returned every time. For some strange reason that I have since come to understand and will explain, the rational part of my brain was no match for the illusion I was chasing.

Then by fluke or whatever mystical reason (okay, desperation), while I was using EFT on what seemed like an unrelated issue, I bumped up against my compulsion to please my deceased father at the expense of my emotional freedom. I realized that even the grave is no match for old, irresistible longings. There while tapping, I uncovered a revelation that was neither new nor earth-shattering, but which emerged as things often do when tapping, in a fresh and clear way: if I try hard enough and succeed at folding the egg whites in just right, everything in my life will be light and airy. Dad's eyes will sparkle for me just as they'd done for Miss Montana. My parents' arguments wouldn't border on explosive; I wouldn't have a stutter; Gigi, my beloved pet, would live forever; and I would finally feel good enough.

Through tapping, I effectively confronted the fact that Dad was being himself, and it was I who was overreaching. Overreaching might have been okay for the first 80,000 times I twisted myself inside out. After all, what little girl doesn't dream of being the apple of her parent's eye? But there is something self-defeating about keeping it going indefinitely. When I saw with my emotional eyes how I was abandoning my own innocence, earnestness, spontaneity, and yes, inner beauty, the kind that comes from appreciating my own tender heart, I was finally able to step in. I allowed my adult self to look at younger, smaller me more through the eyes of Glinda the good witch and less through the lens of an unreasonable, unforgiving drill sergeant.

And yet as I write this, I confide in you that my inner Miss Inadequacy is firing up. No surprise. The prospect of sharing (exposing) my shitty first draft, so titled by author and teacher, Anne LaMott, in her *New York Times* best-seller, *Bird by Bird*, is making me mildly queasy. "Perfectionism," she describes, is "the voice of the oppressor, the enemy of the people. It will keep you cramped and insane your whole life." The cramp, she explains, is what happens when a psychic muscle "cramps up around our wounds—the pain from our childhood, the losses and disappointments of adulthood, the humiliations suffered in both—to keep us from getting hurt in the same place again, to keep foreign substances out." And so the cramping around this shitty first draft comes over me here, with countless rewrites still ahead. There is no telling when or if the final draft will ever be good enough. The tightening around the tender heart of my chipped-toothed middle-schooler fearful that Dad and you, his understudy, will lob one of those "You'll never be's . . ." in my direction is all too familiar.

Does this bother me? To be perfectly honest, it does. But less so than it would have had I not peeled back the layers of my own character onion. I would have continued to believe that what defines my "enoughness" is his approval. And yours.

To my well-intentioned, overprotective, and obnoxious drill sergeant, I can now (often, if not always) say:

> "Sir, it does not.
> I am enough.
> I was enough.
> I have always been enough.
> Now get lost."

# CHAPTER 9

## Psychological Masks and the Faces of Our False Self

You can see that our social masks, our personas, were not created randomly. They were developed in response to events and circumstances that led us to compensate for our perceived shortcomings in specific ways. If we felt intellectually inferior, we may have adopted a mask of "know-it-all." If we felt flawed or inadequate, perhaps we constructed a mask of "perfectionist." If we doubted whether we were wanted, we might have donned the mask of "overachiever" or "prover." If we felt sad, depressed, or frightened, a cover of "all is well" might be what hides the shame we carry for feeling weak.

As a psychotherapist who specializes in self-esteem, my focus is on helping people identify their masks so that they can begin to disassemble them. Not because they are bad but because they are limiting. By having the courage to understand exactly what shame-based secret identity our masks are covering, my clients, you, and I all have the chance to face the reality of our past, honor our young selves for all we've been through, and discover the deepest respect for the core of who we are. Only then can our shame be purged, our authenticity restored, and our rights redefined. Each of us can finally grow up, beyond our childhood pain.

To do this and to grow in self-confidence, it is necessary to expose the pretenses we hide behind, the disguises we use to conceal our shame. Note that there is a relatively small number of psychological masks that exist, since most of us share basic childhood wounds. But there are countless variations and combinations of these masks. Being able to see past our exterior features—beyond the cute, bullying, passive, pouncey, helpless, controlling, smarty-pants, meek, aggressive, seductive, buttoned-up, sarcastic, beige, boisterous, loud, frenetic, withdrawn, too humorous, too humorless, crass, rigid, flighty, overly generous, stingy aspects of ourselves requires a willingness and commitment to explore everything we are and everything we're afraid we are. Only by admitting and accepting the totality of our humanness, regardless of how unappealing we think it is, can we stop investing precious time and energy in running away from ourselves. Only when we turn around and look to the east for the sunrise can we experience the brilliant, golden nature of our spirit.

Naturally you can choose not to embark on this sobering journey of self-awareness. But if you want to know how you got to be the person you are, why you behave the way you do, why you seem to attract the experiences and people that come into your life, and what you can do to reclaim your authentic nature, I encourage you to reflect on the following masks and see if you recognize any of yours.

As you read through the masks, if you notice a "negative" reaction in yourself, take note if it reminds you of someone whose qualities you strongly object to. Remember that the hallmark of the shadow is to prove that we do not have a certain unlikeable quality by railing against it when we spot it in others. Often, the more intense the negative reaction, the greater the possibility that there is something about that unacceptable trait that hits close to home. Our denial would have us believe that we are completely free of the offending trait while someone else has it 100 percent. We are wearing the opposite mask to prove that we are not that, or we are wearing the exact same mask and are simply too blinded by denial to recognize it. Either way, our unconscious sets out to prove we are not what we despise in others.

By exploring the subtleties of our masked selves and understanding the shame and vulnerability that gave rise to it, we can find what we buried long ago. Our lost self rather than our idealized self, once recovered, takes us out of denial and past the places where we are stuck.

## Trauma

We cannot explore psychological masks without mentioning trauma. Emotional trauma has been the subject of widespread research across various disciplines, i.e. children who were either forced into or trapped within an abusive relationship where they had no escape from a frightening or neglectful caregiver, or who witnessed violence against others were truly victimized. Obviously, children have no control over how their caregivers treat them. Traumatic experiences, especially chronically toxic ones such as being raised in a severely chaotic household or one in which a parent was besieged by rageful outbursts, addiction, or depression, produce psychically devastating results. Never having been taught how to regulate their emotions and soothe themselves, these children grow into adults who do not know how to make themselves feel emotionally safe. Burdened by a lack of self-efficacy skills, the ones necessary to take certain courses of action in life, these individuals are caught in an unresolved trauma state.

With what we now know about trauma, thanks in large measure to researchers such as Boston-based psychiatrist Bessel van der Kolk, one of the preeminent pioneers in the study and treatment of trauma, the developing brains of children who endured it are negatively affected and are themselves encased in a body that has been violated. Trauma, as Dr. van der Kolk explains, is not suffered by soldiers, refugees, or victims of sexual assault alone, the types of people we might typically think of when we think of trauma. Psychological trauma can happen to anyone, and it often does. The trauma caused by childhood physical or emotional neglect, parental addiction to alcohol or drugs, sexual or domestic abuse, migration trauma including events taking place at the border wall at the time of this writing, are examples of trauma. Such stress and strain wreak havoc on and in victims' bodies. Voices that had not been able to protest or scream loudly enough to evade danger or abuse, bodies that have been subjected to harm or utter neglect as a result of malnourishment, under nourishment, or grossly inadequate hygiene, or physical and emotional burdens that overstretched a child's ability to cope all leave their imprint in the body.

We can think of trauma in terms of big and little, though in a literal sense, trauma is trauma. Trauma with an upper case "T," for instance, might refer to "big" traumas: your home is destroyed in a natural disaster, your parent is seriously ill when you are young, or you suffer a serious injury. A "small t" trauma might stem from the time in the sixth grade when you had the lead in the school play and forgot your line. On stage, in front of the whole school you froze and were speechless. All you could do was stare out into the audience, unable to utter a sound. You thought the teasing and embarrassment that followed would never end. It is hard not to wince just thinking about it, still. Both "big T" and "little t" traumas work their way through the body in the same physiological way. Only the degree differs.

Dr. van der Kolk's research in neuroscience has demonstrated that trauma physically affects both brain and body, causing debilitating symptoms of various types: anxiety, deep-seated rage, sleeplessness, muscle constriction, digestive disorders, detachment, and its more extreme expression—dissociation, memory loss, and an inability to concentrate. Patients have trouble remembering and trusting. Forming lasting relationships can feel like an uphill climb. These individuals often feel as though they have lost control of themselves. And in a certain way, they have. Trauma has stolen something precious: the ability to feel connected to oneself.

In his revolutionary book, *The Body Keeps the Score: Brain, Mind and Body in the Healing of Trauma*, Dr. van der Kolk uses brain science to demonstrate that trauma stored in the body must be addressed physiologically. Trauma victims, van der Kolk says, are estranged from their bodies by a series of events that begin deep in the brain. As already noted, when faced with a threat, the amygdala triggers a fight-flight-freeze response, which activates a flood of hormones. This response typically persists until the threat has subsided. But if the threat does not subside, the body's alarm keeps sounding, and the cascade of hormones continues. Such a persistent dispensing of stress chemicals is detrimental to the health of our body and can lead to physical and emotional ailments such as the ones mentioned earlier. In the brain of the trauma victim, the threat trigger is either "stuck" in the "on" position or easily activated at the slightest provocation. It is as though the physiological fire is never fully extinguished. Due to the uncomfortable, in fact, intolerable nature of this experience, patients avoid inhabiting their own bodies. They get away from the internal mayhem by dissociating, that is, taking leave of their bodies so as *not to feel what they are feeling*. Over time, they begin to find ways of numbing themselves altogether. Alcohol, drugs, food, and work are means by which they muffle their physical state. The longer this goes on, the less they can remain present in any given situation. According to van der Kolk and others who discuss embodied therapies, the goal of treatment is to resolve the disconnect. "If we can help our patients tolerate their own bodily sensations, they'll be able to process the trauma themselves." ("A Revolutionary Approach to Treating PTSD," *The New York Times*, May 22, 2014). His approach is aimed at helping patients reconnect their thoughts with their bodies. Only then, he asserts, can trauma survivors gain an inner sense of safety in their bodies, which brings them back to themselves and grounds them in the present moment.

Trauma victims, particularly those who suffered abuse at the hands of a caregiver, were so busy surviving the emotional side of their childhood, on their own, that they did not have the luxury, indeed the right, to know their rights. It did not (and could not) have dawned on them that they were entitled to their own feelings, preferences, and boundaries, because such basic entitlements were not taught to them by the adults in whose care they were raised. They simply never learned that their feelings mattered, much less were to be respected. In fact, they were given the opposite message. The relationship between unresolved trauma, whether big or little, and the psychic numbing provided by the personas we have created, is an intricate one. In some cases, a traumatic event does not lead to prolonged suffering. After an initial period of stress and destabilization, the traumatic event may resolve on its own. The memory may be present, but the emotional impact will be minimal. In many instances, however, the physical manifestations of trauma can exist in our bodies, regardless of whether we are consciously thinking about the traumatic event. Our rational mind may think, *I have a nice life. I have everything that should make me happy. Why, then, don't I feel happy?* In a very real way, our conscious and unconscious minds do not share a common set of facts. Where trauma is concerned, our bodies carry the unspoken burden of quite a different story, and this story is the reason for our unhappiness.

## The Faces of Our False Self

Each of us has a basic nature, a tendency to be either a predator (fight) type or a prey (flight) type of person. Out of this nature and the environmental influences that supported it, our masks are created. Regardless of which type we are, both originate from the way we sought to protect ourselves from harm, from physical or emotional discomfort, from life's adversities, from trauma—the big ones and the little ones.

To gain clarity about your mask, you must be willing to

explore your motives and behaviors to understand who you are beneath the façade you show to the world. To truly be free, you must be able to live in your body. To do that, as I have learned from van der Kolk and others, you must be shown that you can befriend your body again, gradually, systematically, and safely. You can use your understanding of your mask together with your bodily sensations to open the door to the truth of who you are, what you've been through, and how you came to form the identity you have. By embarking on this journey, you will likely discover options for living that you never imagined. Constraining beliefs can dissolve. Emotional walls can be let down a little at a time. Stuck energy can move, and creativity can flow once again. Healing and integration of our false self and our wounded self can finally begin to take place.

What follows is a description of psychological masks. We look at some of the more commonly worn ones, the "language" of each one, what each looks like in day-to-day interactions, what the wearer feels and hides from, and what must be faced in order to achieve integration. You will notice some overlap among the masks. This is for two reasons. First, trauma undermines a basic sense of safety shared by all who experience it, and second, sufferers share a common goal: to protect themselves from feeling pain.

See whether you recognize any of your own masks. We typically wear at least two, the one we show outwardly and the one we wear when no one is looking. If you feel that you are triggered as you read these descriptions, please exercise good judgment and take care of yourself. Taking responsibility for your own well-being is the kindest and smartest thing you can do for yourself. Please do not hesitate to take a break from reading. When you feel calmer and ready, only then should you continue reading. If you still feel uneasy, it could mean that something very meaningful is being stirred up for the purpose of becoming released. In that case, I encourage you to consult a certified EFT practitioner for support. You can obtain a list of practitioners in your area by going to www.thetappinsolution.com. While no one can breathe, think, or do your inner work for you, it does not mean you have to do it alone.

### The Mask of the People Pleaser

The Mask of People Pleaser projects an image of "easy to get along with," "super accommodating" and "easily able to figure out what is expected of them."

*Language:*
"Whatever you want."
"I don't know, you decide."
"Whatever makes you happy."

**Question:** What could possibly be the drawback of getting along easily with others? Being nice, even accommodating? How can letting others decide what to do, where to go, or how to proceed possibly be a problem?

**Answer:** When you are driven to make others happier than you make yourself.

What this mask looks like:

- Giving in
- Conforming

- Indecisive
- Compliant

*Motto:* "Don't make waves."

*What message it sends to others:* You live to please others. You have very few needs of your own.

### The Façade

This mask conceals an underlying fear that tending to one's own needs will alienate others. As such, People Pleasers are overly worried about appearing selfish and compensate for this by being highly attuned and responsive to the needs of others.

As children, People Pleasers received the message that they were loved when they satisfied their parents' wishes or made their lives easier. These expectations may have been communicated consciously or unconsciously, overtly, or subtly. Because they were rewarded when they did bend to such wishes, chastised, or withdrawn from when they didn't, budding People Pleasers concluded that the best way, perhaps the only way, to hold onto this love was to fulfill their parents' expectations. To this end, they tend to be agreeable as often as they can and will do almost anything to avoid confrontation. Regardless of what it required, and it often required censoring and editing their truer nature, children who have grown to be People Pleasers can seldom recall instances when their own emotional needs were looked after. These dutiful children, while having their material needs met, experienced more of a one-way street where their emotional needs were concerned. They developed skills such as chameleonizing—being what they thought others wanted them to be—skills that became absorbed into their personality.

What began as a specific way of coping with a specific circumstance or event grew into a generalized way of being. By shaping their behavior and customizing their feelings to fit the mold of what was expected of them, the People Pleaser's boundaries and sense of self were often overshadowed by other peoples' requirements. Their own needs, wants, and feelings went unmet. As a result, People Pleasers are frequently unaware of what they need to feel fulfilled. Their own emotions, feelings and inner landscape are virtual unknowns. Without this self-knowledge, People Pleasers are left without crucial data with which to live their lives.

### How the People Pleaser Feels

People Pleasers tend to harbor a deep sense of personal doubt. They feel some measure of unworthiness, emotionally empty without the approval and acceptance of others to fill them up. Mostly out of touch with this unconscious feeling state, they feel compelled to give and over-give, often to the point of exhaustion. When their over-giving is not reciprocated or when their rare requests for help are either unnoticed or declined, these individuals suffer crushing disappointment and intense resentment. They "ask for so little after all," and are incredulous when their pleas (usually expressed as hints) go unsatisfied. Their currency is their time as much as their money and their sense of fulfillment is derived from making others happy. On a deeper level, People Pleasers are terrified of being pushed away, abandoned, or left behind. A tireless pattern of over giving is one way that these otherwise good-hearted individuals defend themselves against hurt or disappointment, their generosity used as a type of insurance policy against rejection.

Those who wear this mask are psychologically fed by the indebtedness, gratitude, and recognition of others. Despite their outward generosity, which is unquestionably sincere, they use their giving to elicit what they deeply crave: validation, self-worth, and belonging.

### What They Hide

"I don't feel good enough or deserving on my own, the way I am. I am worthwhile only if I can make others happy. I am nothing special or valuable. It is my giving that gives me value."

### The Turnaround

To loosen this persona, individuals who wear the Mask of People Pleaser must first recognize the mechanism by which they have been masking their deepest self. They must be willing to consider how their giving has been a cover, in part, for what they desperately want—being loved for who they truly are—as well as a shield against their lifelong hidden feelings of anger, disappointment, and sadness. By learning to recognize and face the feelings they have neglected by over-focusing on others' needs, they can begin to see how in need they are of their own benevolence. Only then can they reclaim what they have sacrificed for love. Only then can they move closer to an honest relationship with the truth of who they are, which is their undeniable birthright. The more that People Pleasers lean into this deeper truth, the more they will see that stuckness cannot maintain its hold over a self that is sufficiently aware of its own workings. Only then can they finally say goodbye to the ingrained belief that they must earn and then prove their worth.

## The Mask of Victim

The Victim often sees him/herself as being on the receiving end of either bad luck or other people's negativity. Feeling "done to," they often fail to see their own participation, large or small, in the creation of their unfortunate circumstances. They find themselves entangled in disagreeable situations repeatedly but have no idea how they got there or how to exit gracefully. The Victim persona illustrates how its wearers unwittingly place themselves in the path of abuse, whether it stems from others or from themselves.

### Language
"Can you believe that happened to me, again?"
"How did this happen?"
"Why me?"

**Question:** What is the problem with looking for sympathy? Doesn't everyone deserve support when something bad has happened?

**Answer:** Of course. Except when the need for almost constant support and reassurance arises more from situations that could (and should) be avoided, and less from circumstances over which the person has no control.

### What Message It Sends to Others
You will be seeking attention from them in the form of pity or agreement, for your perceived misfortune.

### The Facade

This mask conceals hidden feelings of helplessness, power-lessness, and resignation, feeling states that are associated with psychological injury or pain. Victim identity revolves around an unconscious preoccupation of what was done to them. This makes perfect sense because things were indeed done to them, most likely in childhood, things over which they had no control. In the Victim's mind, they are as pow-erless today as they were then, when they were hurt or ne-glected, by someone in authority and/or someone they loved, and had no way out.

Quite possibly, the only semblance of nurturance these children received came in the form of sympathy from pe-ripheral adults, i.e., teachers, neighbors, or even Child Pro-tective Services. Never having been taught how to regulate their emotions and soothe themselves, these children grew into adults who do not know how to make themselves feel emotionally safe. Burdened by a lack of self-efficacy skills, the ones necessary to take certain courses of action in life, and an overreliance on sympathetic responses from others, these individuals are caught in an unresolved trauma state. Unable to ask for what they need or unaware of what it is they need, they give in to others (whether others expect them to) and then secretly feel resentful when their sacrifices go unnoticed or unrewarded. Rather than reevaluate the usefulness of this pattern, those with a Victim persona tend to double down on their effort, hoping that next time the outcome will be differ-ent. Addicted to getting agreement for their struggle and their victimhood, they keep reinvesting in their efforts, hoping for a satisfying payoff. Not unlike the gambler who continuously puts money in the slot machine, hoping that the next pull will bring in the jackpot, the Victim spends his or her emotional resources of time and energy (as well as the time and energy of others) chasing validation in this way.

Their disappointment in themselves is projected outward as blame toward others for not considering their feelings. Their endless storytelling about how used, manipulated, or slighted they feel has become their misguided and futile plea for attention and affirmation. Feeling loved only when they receive sympathy from others, these individuals walk around with deep unhappiness even if they appear content. Often well put together, Victim personas wear another mask that sends a temporary signal that they are "fine."

Sadly for the Victim, the need for sympathy is never quite satisfied. Listeners of the Victim's stories see right through their disguise and usually sense that they can never offer enough agreement or comfort to satisfy the Victim's insatiable appetite. It is much more obvious to onlookers that the Victim persona is attracted to the kind of familiar drama that was endured in childhood and seems to walk toward it, whereas other personas would turn around and run in the other direction. Such is the unfortunate outcome of an early life where the seeds of trauma were sown.

### How the Victim feels

Those with a Victim persona feel safest when their need for validation is met *vis-à-vis* the pity others take on them along with agreement that they have been unfairly treated. As we have seen, they yearn for outside attention and fail to see what is valuable about themselves. Instead, they feel they can only be recognized for their attention-worthy victimization. This persona is only reinforced by the sympathetic reactions of others which keeps the pattern going. The cycle continues even as people tire of listening to the endless litany of woeful accounts. When the Victim loses his or her listeners, they react with more victimization. Eventually they simply move on to find a new, sympathetic ear.

### What would be revealed if their mask were to be lifted

Beneath the Victim's mask lies both excruciating emotional pain and a simultaneous disconnection from this pain.

"I don't feel worthy of having my real needs met. I don't know what my real needs are. I don't really know who I am if I'm not my (sad, pitiful, unjust) story."

### Underlying Belief About Self

Wearers of this mask believe they must conceal their true feelings or else something bad will happen. Accustomed to suppressing their authentic emotions, Victims have become strangers to their truer, deepest selves. They walk around emotionally detached from their feelings toward the people who originally hurt them.

### Link to the past

The Victim would benefit by taking a difficult but crucial look into their early life to explore when they may have been victimized in some way by someone they loved and/or depended upon, or someone who was in a position of authority. Unprotected and vulnerable, the Victim likely responded in one of two ways: they froze because they were too young and helpless to defend themselves, or they "went along with," realizing that by being passive they could minimize further harm or damage. Their childhood helplessness, which was entirely understandable and reasonable back then, extended into adulthood and now shows up as a pattern of passivity. This current stance, which manifests in thoughts such as, "Well, what can I do?," "I don't know what to do about my problem," "I can't do anything about it," is really expressing a hesitancy, a fear, or a resistance to change. That is because on a deep level, the ability to stand up for themself has been virtually untested. If the Victim persona does want to stand up for herself, she simply does not feel safe enough to do so. As is the case with every human being, safety is the number-one priority.

Passivity and helplessness in adulthood disguise past and present emotions, such as anger or deep pain, disappointment, or hurt. The fear of expressing these emotions can be so strong that doing nothing—as self-defeating as that is— seems the better choice. Staying stuck in life, though painfully frustrating on a conscious level, is preferable on a subconscious level. This is the deep conflict that is masked by this and other personas. In the recesses of the Victim's mind, it is wiser and safer to remain "frozen" in time rather than to look at the source of the unhappiness and risk feeling vulnerable, as was the case in childhood. Furthermore, traumatic experiences do not just harm a child emotionally, they also harm the young, developing brain.

Unexpressed feelings from the past remain within us, unprocessed. Much the way improperly metabolized food cannot break down and deliver vital nutrients to the body, unprocessed emotions cannot deliver the ingredients that feed a healthy mind. What does feed a healthy mind is a consciousness that is able to respect the reality of the past without distorting, denying, or dissociating from it. Unmetabolized emotions will inevitably catch up to us and may result in great harm to our relationships as well as to our sense of ourselves, blocking energy, and obstructing flow and harmony.

### The Turnaround

The first step in loosening the tight seal of the Victim mask is for its wearers to face the ways in which they have participated, knowingly or unknowingly, in the unfortunate circumstances of their life. By taking ownership of their own piece of the problem, those with a Victim persona can start to see the control they have exerted over their own lives. They can trace how things got to be exactly where they are now.

By admitting their fair share of the outcome, these individuals can begin to undo the belief that they are powerless, and instead, take note of the authority they have had over the direction of their lives. The origin of their negative patterns can be traced to the core events and significant people in their lives and linked to the traumatic event, circumstances, or memories that took root long ago. *By bringing the Victim's attention to bodily sensations that store and express the imprint of trauma, the ingrained perception that the world is a dangerous place within which they have no say can be reinterpreted.* The fight, flight, freeze mechanism, which is housed in the recesses of the brain and inaccessible by talk therapy alone, can be reset with an embodied therapeutic approach (See EFT for masks in a later section) in an atmosphere of empathic attunement and non-judgment. The feedback loop between body and brain that has plagued the Victim for years, can be interrupted.

## The Mask of "I'm fine"

The Mask of "I'm fine" projects an image of "all's well," regardless of what is going on in one's life.

### What This Mask Looks Like:

Overly eager to connect.
Overly familiar.
Upbeat and over-the-top friendly.

### What This Mask Sounds Like:

"It's all good."
"I'm okay."
"I'm fine."

**Question:** What is wrong with feeling "fine"? How can always being upbeat and problem-free be a problem?

**Answer:** When it is a cover for unwanted feelings and a veneer that conceals a truer self.

### The Façade

"I'm fine" people walk around as if they are on a television sitcom. They are perpetually amped up, intense, and exaggerated. Their behavior can be excessively animated, and their volume is frequently turned all the way up. These individuals tend not to sense the atmosphere of a room as they enter it. Their interpersonal dial is stuck on hyper-enthusiastic. Whatever they express, they express with exponential and often disproportionate intensity. Regardless of what they are really feeling, wearers of this mask have only one speed: things are "great."

When things do go south from time to time, "I'm fine" individuals maintain an outward appearance that they are unflappable, even "above" such emotions as sadness or overwhelm. They steel themselves against such feelings to remain unfazed or at least to look like they are. They are convinced that the way to feel accepted by others is to be the humorist or life of the party. Some would say they are perpetually running for mayor. Others might see them as high maintenance or exhausting to be around.

### What They Hide

The "I'm fine" persona consists of a psychological glaze that covers a lifetime of sadness, hopelessness, disappointment, anger, and hurt. Feeling safest when they can portray an imperturbable front and a self-possessed image, this group protects themselves against their "down" feelings by constantly lightening things up. Often unaware of the anger and disappointment that exist below the surface, they seek relief from pent-up emotions via covert, subtle, and less-direct measures of rebellion such as "forgetting" appointments or commitments. They frequently keep their unhappiness veiled beneath jokes and comedic performances, alcohol, or drugs.

If their "fine" disguise were peeled back, what would be revealed is a person who is anything but. They were children whose pleas and needs for nurturance often went unheard. Frustrated and let down, these children intuitively understood that their appeals were to no avail. They instinctively reacted to this ongoing dynamic with a type of inner resignation that said, "What's the use? No one is listening. No one cares."

Using their personality mask to camouflage their vulnerable feelings, they are invested in looking flawless to the world.

More fundamentally, they seek to maintain this appearance even to themselves. Deep down, they are terrified that if they allow their seamless facade to crack, the fissure could easily become a fault line. The stark division between the part of themselves they judge and detest and the part that they prefer to identify with would no longer hold. Their most profound worry is that if they permit even the slightest bit of fear or negativity to leak through their barrier, they will be completely overcome. "If I start to cry, I'm afraid I will never stop."

### The Turnaround

The wearers of the "I'm fine" mask have an opportunity, and indeed, a calling to face the realities of their inner selves. Rather than bury their disappointment and anger under a layer of flawlessness, the "I'm fine" person deserves the support to look beneath their polished exterior to the heart of their pain. The more they face the truth of those times during their young lives when they were anything *but* fine, the less they will feel the need to hold it all in. They can take that on because they are safe now, free from parental wrath, neglect, or anything else that stifled the truest expression of their authenticity. These tenderhearted mask wearers can remove the calluses that formed around their vulnerable core and they can finally grant themselves permission to be who they really are now—and who they have been all along.

## The Mask of Apologizer

The Mask of Apologizer projects an image of "It's my fault."

### Language

"I'm sorry."
"I'm sorry."
"I'm sorry."

**Question:** How could apologizing be a problem? Especially if you have done something to hurt or offend someone else?

**Answer:** It's not. Unless you apologize for things that are clearly not your fault, not within your control or are otherwise undeserving of an apology.

### What It Looks Like

If someone bumps into you, you say, "I'm sorry." If you ask someone for the time, you begin with, "I'm sorry." If you are offended by someone else's offense, you apologize. You apologize for apologizing.

### What Message It Sends to Others

You will accept blame not only for your actions but for the actions of others. You need reassurance that you are okay.

### The Façade

This mask conceals an underlying belief that its wearer is wrong, could be wrong, was wrong for something, anything, everything.

### How the Apologizer Feels

The inward life of the Apologizer is a low-grade hell. Feeling tentative and undeserving of positive attention, these individuals are perpetually braced for being told that they are inadequate somehow or have done something to mess up. Because they are unaware of exactly what that might be (everything is potentially their fault), they safeguard themselves in the bubble wrap of apologies. This preemptive "admission" cushions their already bruised egos against criticism from others. The apology is a veiled plea for forgiveness.

### The Reveal if this Mask Were to Be Lifted

Beneath their mask, Apologizers feel a profound sense of unworthiness and emotional isolation. They likely experienced a long time ago that their very presence, their needs, feelings, perceptions were too much, too intense, or too wrong to be met. Unable to see that perhaps their caregivers were limited in their ability to provide adequate emotional support and guidance, these children grew into adults who are convinced that their very existence is a burden.

Apologizers never quite know why they feel as lonely as they do. Their hesitant, unsettled persona belies their often-high intelligence. They try hard to problem-solve their way out of their unhappiness but because the root is outside their awareness, they come up solutionless. Under their ginger exterior is a person who is ashamed and even frightened by the anger they carry. They feel as though the weight of the world is on their shoulders, and they feel cheated of the validation they rightfully deserved in childhood. It is typical for Apologizers to be hard on themselves, taking the unconscious anger that they feel toward key figures in their lives and turning it back on themselves, becoming depressed.

### Underlying Belief About Self

"I feel less than."

"If people saw the real me, they would see what I see. They would see how inadequate I am."

### The Turnaround

Apologizers must acknowledge the fact that it is they who have felt let down by significant people in their lives. They must recognize that while they have been the ones to apologize profusely, deep down they are the ones who are owed an apology. Their caregivers, however unintentional, failed them. It is highly unlikely that the Apologizer will receive the apology he or she deserved, and I am not suggesting that they wait for one. In many cases, the caregiver may be deceased. What the Apologizer must do however is confront the fact that their exterior of "it's my fault" conceals a deeper truth and a heartbreaking disappointment that some things were the fault of others and not likely to be rectified.

The Apologizer can be guided to come to terms with the futility of waiting for an apology. By understanding what they deserved and putting words to it, these individuals can shift from a life of emotional tiptoeing to one in which they embrace their basic emotional rights. This will result in the Apologizer seeing herself or himself on more equal footing with others, something that has been deeply yearned for but sorely missing until now.

### The Mask of Over-Competence

The Mask of Over-Competence projects an image of all-out capability.

## Language

"I know how."

"It's already done."

"I can do it better than most.

**Question:** Sounds perfectly fine, right? What could be the drawback of being competent?

**Answer:** Nothing, except when your need to "be this way" stems from a fear that behaving in any other fashion is unacceptable and even emotionally dangerous. This fear leads to a compulsion that one must always oversee everything which can result in the inevitable feelings of burnout and resentment.

## What This Mask Looks Like

Extreme self-reliance

## The Message It Sends to Others

You are always the "go-to" person. You rarely, if ever, need help and you certainly do not go asking for it if you do.

## The Façade

This mask hides a deep-seated neediness for which its wearers feel ashamed and wrong. Their shame is accompanied by an equally deep sense that needing anything from others is a futile endeavor, since they are certain to be disappointed.

## How the Overly Competent Person Feels

The Overly Competent persona portrays an exterior of mastery over life's logistical, organizational, and strategic challenges. Exceptional problem-solvers, the individuals who don this mask are disguising a deeply held belief that their emotional needs are too overwhelming for anyone to meet. This was indeed their early life experience and their fierce independence and self-reliance reflect this. On an unconscious level, the long-standing accumulation of unfulfilled needs feels both overwhelming and frightening. Their shame-based identity is one in which they feel fundamentally flawed, broken, sick, unwanted. They become profoundly uncomfortable with the slightest hint of emotional vulnerability and pride themselves on not needing anyone.

### The Reveal if the Mask Were Lifted

The Overly Competent individual is terrified of emotional exposure and has mastered the ability of going through life successfully dodging it. Placed in the untenable position of having to deny any semblance of neediness to cope with profound frustration as a child, this persona camouflages, among other things, an almost insatiable emotional emptiness and self-reproach. Because this emptiness factored so prominently in the young psyches of this group, Overly Competent men and women ward off the discomfort of emotional hunger by turning to addictive obsessions that ease—at least temporarily—the ache of unsatisfied longing. This often shows up, but is not limited to, uncontrollable overeating. Other addictive behaviors such as compulsive shopping, internet, substance abuse, or gambling may also be used to dull the sensation of an inner void.

### The Link to The Past

Overly Competent adults were once needy children who were hard pressed to understand why their basic and legitimate emotional needs went unattended. Like the other masks, this one was constructed to lessen the pain associated with a persistent, intangible psychic void. Many wearers of this mask had to contend not only with this hole but with at least one caregiver whom they had to emotionally parent. What resulted was a child in need of nurturance, guidance, and protection who not only received too little herself but was then expected (demanded) to turn around and provide these to an insatiable adult.

Often bright and resourceful, these children's young capacities were stretched beyond their ability and they somehow managed to think and behave like big boys and girls way before it was appropriate for them to do so. Among the most troubling implications of this lies in the fact that even their best efforts could not elicit what they most needed and longed for from their caregiver: protection, nurturance, guidance. As a result, these children sadly experienced subjective feelings of failure and inadequacy. The relative insufficiency of the caregiver, which was likely unintentional and due to psychological or physical ills, grief, or arrested development, produced a double-edged personality trait in the affected children. On one hand, they grew up with the belief that it is their sole responsibility to oversee almost everything in their lives, that it is not safe or prudent to depend on others, and frankly, because they are so good at it, it is their job to constantly take charge and make others' lives easier. On the other, they have no frame of reference for accepting care and support. Their pride for getting by on extraordinarily little, coupled with their natural inclination to focus on others, leaves the Overly Competent person walled inside an existence of extreme self-sufficiency. They simply cannot believe (trust) that anyone is both interested in and capable of loving them for who they are. Their personal sense of value is tied up in how well they take care of others, but they seldom, if ever, feel as though they are anything but used. While the Overly Competent person wants nothing more than to feel accepted, they live with the belief that if anyone were to discover how enraged and sad they really feel, they would undoubtedly be cast aside. Therefore, their primary way of feeling loved is to keep providing for others which keeps them feeling used.

### The Turnaround

Individuals who wear the Mask of Overly Competent can get to their sunrise, but they must do a few things first. These steps will surely seem counterintuitive, but they offer a pathway out of the vicious cycle just described. First and foremost, they must admit that they were emotionally alone as a child. Next they will need to admit that they have been craving closeness, care, and attention, and did so when they were young and truly dependent. They must then face their lifelong yearning to have been special to someone, most especially to their caregiver, before they shut down this need in utter disappointment and despair.

In the space between the craving and the aloneness is the opportunity to heal this wound. If they are willing to connect with the part of themselves that felt vulnerable, let down, helpless, and wanting, they will see that they survived it all once before and they can survive the memory of it now. They are no longer young, trapped victims. They have car keys, their own apartments, and the power to say "no." They can take the brave step of seeing that they no longer need to keep themselves shut down in order to keep the pain away. They can face the pain they have already endured without sacrificing their life force and their emotional vitality. They can begin to come alive again. In taking this step, they will feel, firsthand, the futility of filling their emptiness with compulsive activities and can instead respond to their childhood neglect with the truthful, respectful, and accurate recognition of their own needs. This does not change what happened, of course. It changes the way the facts of what happened *are dealt with*. As they handle the addictions that have amplified their shame, they can be more attuned to their inner needs rather than mute them. They can connect emotionally to what it is they have been starving for all along and feed themselves the kind, compassionate, and competent attention they deserve. Their own.

## The Mask of Avoidance

Staying away from feelings, circumstances, or situations that are emotionally painful is the function of the Mask of Avoidance. It is typically used against overwhelming feelings, such as anger or profound disappointment.

### Language (*spoken or unspoken*)
"I was so furious, I just walked away."
"I was so hurt; I just didn't say a word."

**Question:** What is the drawback of walking away or cooling off, especially when you are feeling angry, hurt, or disappointed?

**Answer:** Well, nothing, and in some instances, it may be a good idea. What is relevant here is that walking away, remaining silent, withdrawing, throwing something, or punching something are behaviors, not the emotion itself. Often when describing strong emotions, many people describe the defense mechanism(s) they use to deal with the feeling, rather than the feeling itself. These statements do not explain how angry or sad you were and why; they describe *what you did* in reaction to your emotion. When avoidance is overused in this way, it may prevent you from getting to the core of your feeling, thereby impeding your ability to examine important issues in your life. This is not to suggest in the slightest that acting out anger is advantageous. Rather, making the conscious distinction between the feeling and the behavior used to conceal it is important if one wishes to understand how emotions and defenses work.

Another method of staying away from upsetting or unacceptable feelings is to keep your distance from other people. Withdrawing or isolating from others is a way of shielding yourself from the challenges that naturally accompany human relationships. Doing so is obviously a barrier to intimacy and can lead to loneliness and significant emotional withdrawal. Avoidance is a mask that can often go undetected by others, since it is usually couched within another mask or defense mechanism, such as rationalization.

"I don't have the time to call her back."

"I'm busy doing something more important than taking the class."

Avoidance itself can show up in other forms, as well. Sarcasm, tantrums, and drama are methods by which some individuals deflect their emotions. Since these traits are difficult to be around, these avoidant tactics successfully distance other people. Emotional separation is thereby achieved, and the Mask of Avoidance manages to keep its wearer isolated with a subjective feeling of safety. In other words, emotional safety is found only by remaining isolated from other people.

## *Cover Up*

There are two kinds of anger. One is appropriate as the response to an attack or threat, and the other stems from an internal emotional conflict, from a sense of hurt or inadequacy. The first kind is justified and rooted in the need to protect oneself, or literally defend one's safety. The profound instinct toward self-preservation ensures survival. When channeled appropriately, anger can prompt behavior that is constructive. It can maximize the chance for physical survival as well as correct social ills. The Civil Rights Movement and the abolition of slavery are two examples of justifiable anger channeled for the benefit of social justice and moral reconciliation. The second kind is defensive in nature. It exists to provide a temporary boost of power, covering up a deeper feeling of powerlessness. It is rage that is unjustified and exaggerated in its intensity. Disproportionate to the offending action, defensive anger is often *displaced*, meaning it is aimed at a target that is thought to be safer and less apt to retaliate or induce guilt. A person who harbors deep anger toward a deceased parent, for example, may find it easier to vent his anger at another driver on the road instead of coming in touch with anger toward the parent for harsh treatment years before. The road rage is an expression of anger that has been misdirected from the true source to a person completely unrelated to the situation. Note however that anger toward the now-deceased parent is itself a cover for deeper feelings of hurt and disappointment where the parent is concerned. In this example, we see the layering of two defense mechanisms: defensive anger and displacement.

To put it succinctly, what the Mask of Avoidance conceals is the true experience of an underlying emotion.

### The Turnaround

Individuals who wear the Mask of Avoidance can find their authenticity only when they are able to contact their truest emotions. Facing painful emotions rather than running away is the action of a psychologically mature adult who understands both the consequences of avoiding emotions as well as the benefits of acknowledging them directly. Because most of us were not taught appropriate ways to express anger, we live in fear of it. Convinced that something terrible will happen if we express our angry thoughts and feelings—either we will encounter someone else's wrath, or we will be overwhelmed, lose control, and explode—we deny the existence of it. We equate verbalizing anger with acting on it. Expressing anger does not mean becoming volatile. A simple statement such as, "I'm upset with the way you spoke to me," can be an appropriate way to let someone know how you feel. If unable to express anger appropriately, it is easy to get stuck in resentment or victimization. Where anger toward parental figures is concerned, it is essential to look beneath the surface layer to see what deeper emotion exists. If someone we love abandons or rejects us, it hurts to the core. Of course, this is a difficult thing to bear. To compound matters, such treatment can suggest to our psyche that we deserved to be abandoned or rejected, that we are to blame for it, or we are somehow unqualified to be loved.

If on the other hand, we can see the rejecting person in the context of his or her history, life experiences and circumstances, we can view whatever treatment we received in a more balanced way. We can eventually say to ourselves, "What a pity that Mom couldn't open her heart to me. How sad it is that she deprived both herself and me the chance to be close, to know the special gift of a loving mother-daughter relationship. I feel sad for myself, and I feel sad for her." By feeling into these words, we allow ourselves to be impacted by them without the stigma or judgment that it was our fault she acted the way she did. In this way, we permit the grief to move through us, mentally and viscerally. By pairing our understanding of Mom with our own genuine, undefended reaction of sadness, we move through the anger to pain and through the pain to an acceptance, which can then be put into perspective.

## The Mask of Rescuer, Fixer

The Mask of Rescuer projects an image of "I'm always available, no matter what."

"What do you need?" is the calling card of the people who wear this persona.

### What this mask looks like

Unlimited availability. No limits on giving and caregiving. You will make time for everyone else, somehow. You never need help yourself.

*Question:* What could be the drawback of always being available to help or to rescue someone? How can generosity and an eagerness to help possibly be a problem?

**Answer:** When rescuing others is done at the expense of rescuing yourself.

### The Façade

This mask covers up an underlying need to be needed. The rescuer's sense of herself is derived from helping others in jams, predicaments, and those at a loss for how to help themselves. Genuinely sensitive and empathic, the rescuer's compulsive need to save others is driven by deeper psychological forces that go beyond generosity and altruism.

Her self-esteem rises and falls on how needed she feels she is. The rescuer is attracted to people who tend toward helplessness, fragility, or neediness, and/or to professional pursuits which require an inordinate amount of attention, often to the point of physical and emotional fatigue. It is this type of rescuing which, despite being overwhelming, provides the Rescuer with a much-needed dose of self-worth.

The exact nature of how and why Rescuers do what they do can be very varied. Most come to this role earnestly. People with this persona often have a history of loss, abandonment, or trauma. Due to the grief, illness, overwhelm, or addiction of a parent or primary caregiver, they were thrust into the role of little hero. Often a child in these circumstances will make astounding attempts to protect and provide for that parent. Moreover, using their heroics was their best hope for optimizing whatever love and parenting the caregiver could provide.

Highly empathic and sensitive, that is, able to understand and identify with the feelings of others, they assumed the role of protector. This protection typically took the form of swallowing her own feelings. This internalizing grew into a way of life for the rescuer who, as an adult, is virtually unable to ask for help, express dissatisfaction or say "no." Consequently, the rescuer lives beneath layers of frustration, resentment, and guilt. Their biggest fear is that they will be exposed as being "needy." As a rule, Rescuers generally don't seek professional help or support unless their ability to "keep all the balls in the air" fails, at which point they become overcome and crushed by their perception that they are a "failure."

### How the Rescuer Feels

Rescuers feel validated, admired, and safe when helping others, but deep within, people with this persona feel an underlying sense of longing and emptiness. Yet they tend to feel highly uncomfortable with their own emotional needs and are generally at a loss for how to respond to them. Giving and over-giving, with no real sense that this is often at the expense of their own well-being, they believe their happiness lies in fixing others, and to a large extent, it does. Deep down however, they secretly yearn to lean on others or to be taken care of. Paradoxically, however, they almost never accept help even when offered. They simply have never exercised their muscle to receive.

### What They Hide

"I wish I could lean on someone. I wish someone would take care of me, for a change."

Like other mask wearers, Rescuers believe their well-being in life depends upon how others see them. They are convinced that they are wanted and valued only if they are doing things for others: favors, problem solving, crisis management, a kidney donation. Their sense of security in relationships is dependent upon and gauged by how well they are meeting others' needs. Swooping in to save the day is their "insurance policy" against being left or left behind. This is the only way Rescuers believe they can maintain closeness or keep the respect and admiration of others. They will do almost anything to make sure they are needed. Unless they are rescuing others or fixing their problems, Rescuers do not believe they are worthy of being liked or loved. "I'm not good enough to be loved exactly the way I am," is the secret mantra of this mask wearer.

### The Turnaround

Rather than relying on rescuing or fixing to compensate for their own feelings of powerlessness and helplessness, Rescuers must acknowledge the truth of their childhood hurts and disappointments and gently move through them. By facing the painful but realistic circumstances of their early life, these mask wearers can disengage from an interpersonal pattern fueled by denial and discover their authentic self. They can trade their compulsive need to fix or save others for a much needed and valuable look within. As they discover that their rock solid "white knight" persona has concealed a tender vulnerability, they are freer to acknowledge what it was they needed emotionally and did not receive. It is precisely within this vulnerability that the missing pieces of a truer self can be found. By taking the time to identify unmet needs, Rescuers can realize that they give to others precisely what they needed themselves but went without. The Rescuer's profound invitation is to see that perhaps the person who most needs rescuing is the Rescuer herself, and she is the only one who can provide it.

# CHAPTER 10

# The Bridge

Each of us adopts a persona that is based on avoiding some aspect of reality that was painful or frightening. This is not an avoidance of the objective facts of our lives (a person may remember, for example, that he never knew when his father was going to come home intoxicated), but more often the avoidance of the *impact* of those facts on our mind and body(this same person may be unaware that the unpredictability of his father's drunken states left him hypervigilant, anxious, and mistrustful of a peaceful moment). In other words, we deny the *emotional consequences* of the reality we have lived through.

Perhaps the single most-important step in getting unstuck and moving forward in life is recognizing that being stuck is not something that happens *to you*. It is something you do internally to keep yourself safe. If you wish to know what that is, you have to increase your self-awareness, observe how you treat yourself in real time—paying attention to the things you say to yourself in your head—and look beneath the mask you've worn for most of your adult life. Only then can you clear up the opaque lens of denial that has been obstructing your vision of yourself and dimming your light.

Most of us were not taught how to turn inward. We do not know how to identify and name our inner experiences. In fact we were encouraged to turn away from them: numb and distract ourselves, project onto others, comfort ourselves with desserts and toys. Beyond this, we may have been taught that going near our internal landscape was pointless, even frightening. In a true sense, we learned to block out a part of who we are. We internalized a message that it is better, safer, to stop being *real* to ourselves. This has left us with a counterfeit recollection of how we became who we are.

To be *real* to ourselves, in a psychological sense, means to fully embrace the totality of who we are, to respect the factual truths of our lives and the emotional truths as well. It means to be integrated in thought, feeling, body, and action. If one does not think it important to cultivate a knowledge of one's own inner workings, one functions in the dark about the factors that influence virtually every choice made in life. This is where it becomes all too easy to look to the outer world and to others to tell us what to think, what to do, and what to feel. When we are not real with ourselves, we run the risk of seeing our identity become impoverished, defined more by others and less by ourselves. We are being who we think we're supposed to be rather than who we are.

The experiences we had with our caregivers and society during our formative years shaped our core beliefs today. We tend not to see these as fluid and flexible but rather as aspects of who we are, a fixed way of being. We simply think that *the way we are* is "just the way we are." Until these hand-me-down beliefs, which became our guiding principles, or more precisely, our *mis*guiding principles, are unpacked, examined, and challenged, we will allow them to dictate our choices and undermine our happiness.

The core beliefs that drive many of our decisions sound something like, "The good things in life . . . they're for other people. They're not meant for me."

"I have to keep the peace in my relationships, even if that means hiding my needs."

"I'm always waiting for the other shoe to drop. It always has."

"Why would he or she want to be with someone like me? I'm not in their league."

Beliefs such as these are halting. They stop us in our tracks.

We are stuck in these beliefs, mistaking them for facts when they are interpretations and adaptations from the past. We conclude that, like the color of our eyes, our thoughts and perceptions are unchangeable. One of the most noteworthy consequences of adhering blindly to our limiting beliefs is the fact that doing so affects ourselves and also those who depend on us. A business partner, for instance, will be held back if her associate cannot envision financial success because of a hidden belief that she does not deserve it. A spouse will be chronically disappointed if his wife is unaware of her belief that she feels unworthy of happiness, and therefore sabotages their marital milestones by going on a major shopping spree, incurring debt every time they seem to get ahead.

Until you look squarely at your programming, you are doomed to repeat it. Hearing this, many of my clients and workshop participants ask what can possibly break a pattern that is as potent, ingrained, and long-standing as this, one that causes them to act against their own interests. My best answer: 1) live mindfully, and 2), practice compassionate recognition. Let's look at the first one here and compassionate recognition a bit later.

*Living mindfully* is about paying attention to yourself. It refers to the voluntary, present, curious, reality-based observation of your inner and outer worlds. It is characterized by a willingness to notice, assess, and integrate information arising from your physical senses, your body, your emotions, your history, your circumstances, and humanity-at-large. Living mindfully relies on your ability to reflect on yourself, to look inward to learn more about your basic nature, inner workings, emotional reactions, and life's purpose. Without self-reflection there can be no self-awareness, and without self-awareness there is little self-knowledge.

The practice of living mindfully requires your openness to seeing beyond your assumptions and a willingness to be mistaken about previously held beliefs, especially ones that resulted from pushing aside your true self. It asks that you stretch beyond your comfort zone, beyond the dual trances of denial and disconnection, and beyond the bounds of what you think you know of yourself. It invites you to reevaluate your limitations, can'ts and won'ts. This willingness to be wrong along with an equal willingness to expand your awareness is exactly what opens the door to a path forward. Confining, closed, limiting thoughts of the past can see new life breathed into them the more willing you are to examine them.

Another exceptionally relevant feature of living mindfully is self-acceptance. Self-acceptance is the willingness to acknowledge *as true* whatever is going on with us at this very moment. This can be a difficult concept to grasp because it can easily be interpreted as approving of everything about ourselves. To some, this may suggest that change or growth is not necessary. On the contrary, self-acceptance is the only effective starting point for change and growth. Why? Because until we face whatever we feel in any given moment, whatever choices we have made, whatever regrets we carry, we will not be able to meet ourselves where we truly are. As long as the truth is concealed by either judgment or denial, we will not be able to touch it. This will make any meaningful change futile because we simply cannot heal from something we do not see.

Clients will often say, "But I can't accept *that* about myself. I hate *that* part of me." Or, "I don't accept myself. That's why I'm here!" Or, "I'm afraid if I say I accept myself, I'm really saying that I will stay the way I am." Acceptance of who we are does not mean we are apathetic to change. If we can heed Popeye's mantra and accept that "I am what I am," and I have said and done and felt the things that I said and did and experienced, then we no longer have to hide behind distortions, delusions, or self-manipulations. We have an unobstructed view of ourselves, maybe for the first time in our lives. This is the starting point for waking up. This is the first clearing of the path out of confusion toward clarity. This is the bridge between the person we think we are supposed to be and the person we truly are. This bridge is within sight.

Self-acceptance, a meaningful and indispensable feature of living mindfully, invites an attitude of self-affirmation, an approach we take in which we tell ourselves we are worth our own time, our own trouble. We uphold what we think and feel without distortion and without waiting for approval. We are willing to tolerate the discomfort of certain truths simply because our psychological maturity depends on it. Facing the reality of our lives instead of running away from it is one of the hallmarks of a successful adulthood. Whereas as children, we may have run outside to play as a means of coping with the unhappiness in our homes, as adults we learn to stand firm and deal with it head on.

In this next chapter we will look at a specific and highly usable method for bridging the gap between the person you have been trying to be—restrained and in control—and the brilliant, messy, tenderhearted, imperfectly good enough person you already are.

As you go through the chapter, look for signs in yourself that can serve as guideposts for working with your own mask. I hope you will see in EFT tapping a realistic, tangible, applicable way for you to discover and reclaim your authenticity. It is time for the real you to shine!

\ \ I / /
## CHAPTER 11
/ / I \ `

# What is Tapping and
# What Can It Do For You?

Emotional Freedom Techniques (EFT), known in simpler terms as tapping, is a self-applied mind/body healing technique that combines the principles of Traditional Chinese Medicine, specifically acupuncture, with contemporary cognitive psychology to reduce the stress response in the body. It is widely understood that the negative effects of cumulative stress on the body can lead to significant emotional and physical symptoms and disease.

## A Brief History of Tapping

Tapping has its roots in what is broadly known as energy therapies. According to the National Center for Complementary and Integrative Health (NCCIH), energy therapies are approaches that seek to rebalance the flow of energy that gets disrupted or "clogged" as it travels along unseen pathways in the body known as meridians. Physical and emotional health, according to proponents of energy medicine, depend upon a smooth and uninterrupted flow of this energy, considered to be an essential life force. One of the basic tenets of traditional Chinese medicine (TCM) is that the body's vital energy (*ch'i* or *qi*) circulates through such meridian channels, which have branches connected to the body's organs and functions.

Contemporary psychology, cognitive behavioral therapy (CBT) in particular, is the study of mental processes including but not limited to perception, memory, memory storage and recovery, and use.

EFT tapping draws its principles from the unique pairing of these two areas. For much of the twenty-plus years during which tapping has been available, the often-impressive results were reported only anecdotally. More recently, scientific research has begun to explain why EFT tapping is so effective and, as several prestigious studies have strongly suggested, its efficacy has much to do with brain function.

Briefly stated, the interplay between and among memory, emotions, bodily sensations, the brain's stress center, and the fight, flight, freeze response is responsible for the way in which traumatic or disturbing events are processed. According to findings by Dr. Peta Stapleton of Australia, who conducts research trials into new therapies, "EFT appears to affect the amygdala (stress center of the brain) and hippocampus (memory center), both of which play a role in the decision process when deciding when something is or isn't a threat . . ." (Stapleton & Sheldon, 2016) by sending a calming signal to that region of the brain.

Here is how it works. During times of acute stress, your amygdala, which has protection as its main goal, sends a powerful distress signal to your body to prepare it to meet the threatening situation. When this "stress center" is switched on, an instantaneous and fascinating sequence of physical events, hard-wired into our survival makeup, becomes mobilized. In a fraction of a second, the amygdala-under-threat produces physiological changes that are designed for bursts of extraordinary physical activity, meant for a single purpose: to help us survive danger.

Functioning much like a control center, this area of the brain communicates with the rest of the body giving us the ability to fight, flee, or freeze in place. Among the most notable of these bodily reactions is the secretion of specific hormones: adrenaline and the primary stress hormone, cortisol. When released, these chemicals prompt a complex sequence of neurobiological events: the heart beats faster than normal, pushing blood to the muscles and other vital organs to maximize speed and strength. Pulse rate and blood pressure increase. Pupils dilate for better night vision. Breathing changes. Small airways in the lungs widen for maximum oxygen intake. Extra oxygen is sent to the brain, increasing alertness. Hearing and other senses sharpen. Digestion slows. Pain is dulled or blocked. Adrenaline triggers the release of blood sugar (glucose) and fats from temporary storage sites in the body which flood into the bloodstream, supplying spare energy. The brain is elevated to red alert and it signals this alert throughout the body.

This intricate and immediate response to danger, whether the danger is real or perceived, occurs so quickly we may not even be aware of it. Even before other areas of our brain can make sense of the threat and well before we can process what is happening, our efficient amygdala has done its job to help us survive. That explains why people can escape the path of an oncoming vehicle even before they think about what they are doing; the powerful surge of chemicals in our body, reacting to commands from the stress center, activates this fear response. Once the threat subsides and the danger has passed, the body calms down and hormone functioning returns to baseline. The same neural wiring that enabled our most vigilant ancestors to survive tiger attacks tens of thousands of years ago by fighting or fleeing helps save our lives today.

As you can see, the amygdala wields a lot of power when it comes to initiating protective split-second physical reactions aimed at predators and other aggressors. In a real sense, it knows before we do when we are in trouble. It constantly scans our experiences, takes in information via our senses and is at the ready to respond to any hint of danger. It is not overly concerned with whether the danger is a tiger on the loose or an angry boss on a tirade, a creepy spider on the ceiling or a creepy person in a movie. Its role is to identify any danger you perceive and then sound the alarm.

## When the stress response is constantly switched "on"

Constantly scanning for danger, the amygdala has much to contend with. Personal stressors combined with unprecedented global ones have many of our amygdalae locked in the "on" position. Good stress catalyzes us to meet goals and deadlines. It can propel us to stretch beyond our comfort zones to empower ourselves and improve our lives. But our scanning amygdala, constantly looking for anything that might indicate potential harm, does not differentiate between situations in which danger is literally present and ones in which we perceive it to be. The spider, though creepy, is not likely to pose much physical harm. However, if your brain associates the insect with a negative or traumatic event, you could develop a fear of spiders. For example, if you saw a spider when you were eight at a family picnic, and you screamed and spilled your soda all over your mom's new blouse, and she yelled at you and remained in a sour mood for hours which in turn caused your dad to storm off in anger, your amygdala might catalog the emotionally upsetting event in the "spider" neuro-file. The "emotional memory" of the charged and unhappy family event becomes linked to the spider sighting. The fear response is triggered without your conscious recollection of the associated event: your parents' squabble and your ensuing guilt.

Our bodies can react in similar fashion to unconscious triggers of all sorts, sending surges of stress chemicals coursing through our systems, preparing us to confront or run away. Stressors of all types, both immediate and anticipated, actual or conjured, layer up in our mind's watchful eye. Global crises, local disasters, and personal challenges combine and require the unmonitored amygdala to flood our bodies with cortisol and other stress hormones. Not good.

Unlike good stress, *distress* causes us to suffer as we get swept up in anxiety and worry, from both internal and external sources, those which we can identify and those we cannot. (The spider part of the girl's story became embedded in her amygdala as an emotional memory, but her parents' angry reaction did not. Her amygdala is operating on only partial information which might be contributing if not causing her to have an excessive fear of spiders.)

One of the interesting features of good stress is that it typically has an outlet. Good stress energizes us and is often tied to a tangible goal. Distress, on the other hand, usually has no outlet. Consequently, there is no release or endpoint for the fight or flight mechanism. The cortisol buildup has nowhere to go and becomes trapped in our biology. Since we cannot control the existence of spiders, for example, any more than we can rejection-proof our lives or bring down the terrorism threat, we exist with cortisol steadily streaming in our body. Persistently elevated cortisol levels interfere with learning and memory, creativity, and problem-solving. They lower immune functioning, increase weight gain, particularly belly fat, raise blood pressure and cholesterol, and are associated with heart disease. Furthermore, chronic stress and high cortisol levels increase the risk for depression, mood instability, and a shorter life expectancy.

There is promising news. Researcher, EFT master trainer, and one of the world's leading experts on energy psychology, Dawson Church, PhD, has conducted several studies in which cortisol levels were measured following exposure to EFT. One landmark randomized controlled trial involving eighty-three subjects compared an hour-long EFT session with an hour of talk therapy. It found that anxiety and depression dropped twice as much with EFT and that cortisol declined by 24 percent in just a single hour (Church, Young, & Brooks, 2012). In his book, *The Genie in Your Genes* (2009), he writes, "When you believe you are under siege, your body has no way of telling that it's just your neurotic mind thinking abstract thoughts. Its old survival system clicks into place."

# The Development of the Tapping Technique

The EFT tapping technique was developed in the 1990s by Gary Craig, a personal performance coach and Stanford University-trained engineer. Streamlined from another method called Thought Field Therapy (TFT) developed by Dr. Roger Callahan a decade before, both approaches maintain that "blocked energy" is responsible for physical and emotional dis-ease. Both rely on "tapping," light percussive touches on meridian points on the face and body, instead of inserting needles, to release the blocked energy. In the Craig method, EFT, fewer points are tapped on, making the process accessible and easy to use while maintaining its effectiveness. A well-respected Harvard study seems to confirm that stimulating key acupuncture points reduces the arousal (stress) response in the brain which brings down the fight, flight, or freeze response immediately triggered when an imminent threat or danger is thought to be present.

# The Mechanics of Tapping

There are five basic steps to tapping:

1.  **Identify the issue**, called a *target*. A target is a memory, an event, a symptom, an emotion, or a bodily sensation that, ***when you think about it now***, causes some disturbance or discomfort in you. The more specific the target, the more beneficial the results.

2. **Rate the degree of intensity** on a scale of 0–10 (10 being maximum).

3. **Create a Setup Statement** that consists of the problem statement coupled with an affirmative coping statement.

4. **Complete a sequence (with Reminder Phrase)**—Completing a sequence means to tap on the acupuncture points while saying the reminder phrase on each point. Tapping gently on each point approximately 7 to 10 times is sufficient. Tapping longer or harder on the points will not affect the results. Finish by letting out a slow, releasing breath.

5. **Re-rate the intensity level**.

This process constitutes one tapping round.

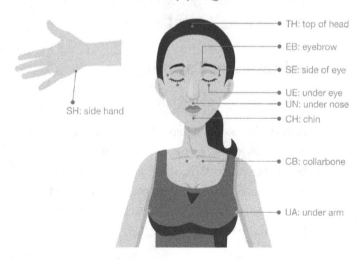

EFT Tapping Points

SH: side hand

TH: top of head
EB: eyebrow
SE: side of eye
UE: under eye
UN: under nose
CH: chin
CB: collarbone
UA: under arm

# How to Tap

EFT tapping follows a specific protocol. You do not need to know or even be concerned for that matter with how or why it works. Knowledge of traditional Chinese medicine, energy healing, cognitive functioning, or brain anatomy is not necessary. This technique works, whether one is aware of the theory which underlies it. You simply need to familiarize yourself and get comfortable with the mechanics which usually takes just a few minutes.

Let's look at the five steps in a bit more detail.

1. *Identify the issue* and focus on whatever is bothering you that you want relief from. This becomes the target at which you "aim" the tapping. When identifying the specific problem or issue you want to work on, keep the following in mind:

   Event: (the time when . . .)

   Emotion: (anger, frustration, anxiety, fear, guilt, emptiness, sadness, jealousy, loneliness, numbness, etc.)

   Belief, such as: *I'm not meant to be happy. Money is for other people. Not me.*

   Memory, such as: *I remember the time they laughed at me.*

   Ask yourself this important question: *How do I know I feel (ex: angry) right now?* (Angry, frustrated, nervous etc.) In other words, where do you feel the feeling in your body when *you think of the target issue now?* Tune into the target issue AND the feeling that arises in your body.

2. ***Rate the initial degree of intensity.*** As you measure your "before" level of intensity, 0–10, look for how strong the feeling of distress is. See if you can pinpoint where you feel it in your body right now, not the way you may have felt in the past or expect to feel in the future, but right now when you call the stressor to mind. Do you notice any physical sensation in your stomach, for example? A sinking feeling or butterflies or churning? Or does your chest feel tight? Do your neck and shoulders tense up? If you don't notice anything, that is okay. You can ask yourself. *How do I know I'm upset right now?* Make a mental note of your number or, better yet, write it down.

3. ***Create a SETUP Statement.*** The setup statement is a phrase that is used to begin each new round of tapping. When devising this phase there are two goals to achieve:

   a. Acknowledge the problem.
   b. Accept yourself despite it.

   We do this by saying:

   "Even though I have this (specific issue), *I accept myself and how I feel.*"

   Insert words in the blank that describe your specific problem.

Some examples:

*This fear of spiders:*

"Even though I have this fear of spiders, *I accept myself and how I feel.*"

*This humiliation when I was twelve when my brother called me fat:*

"Even though I have this humiliation from when I was twelve because my brother called me fat, *I accept myself and how I feel right now.*"

*This foot pain in my left foot:*

"Even though I have this throbbing (sharp, dull, constant, burning) pain in my left foot, *I accept myself and how I feel in this moment.*"

The important reasons we begin with the Setup Statement: First, it brings full awareness to the problem instead of avoiding or suppressing it, which is often the case when one is faced with uncomfortable problems, memories, or feelings. Second, you are telling yourself that although you *have* the problem, *you are not the problem.* Too often, we identify with our difficulties and judge ourselves harshly. It is this self-judgment that is almost as damaging as the problem itself and that keeps us from processing our emotions constructively. The less we process these emotions the more we remain stuck. This step, the Setup Statement, begins to mentally separate you from the problem, to help you dis-identify with it. In this new "space" between you and your problem, some objectivity develops, room to choose differently or see things in a new way.

Let's say you want to address the loud critical voice in your head. You might say something like this:

> "Even though I have this critical voice in my head, *I accept who I am and how I feel.*"

> "Even though I have this critical voice in my head and it's always chattering, *I accept this is where I am right now.*"

> "Even though I have this critical voice in my head, *I accept myself anyway.*"

4. ***Sequence with Reminder Phrases.*** As you tap on the designated points on your face and body, you will use a reminder phrase on each point. The Reminder Phrase is the shorthand version of the longer Setup Statement that is meant to keep you tuned into exactly what you are working on.

   Example: "This critical voice." Tap on each point, and as you do repeat this Reminder Phrase. (Later, once you have learned the foundations of EFT tapping, we can move on to more in-depth setup statements. Many people who are new to tapping report improvement even when using the mechanics in this most basic way.

5. ***Re-rate the degree of intensity*** on a scale of 0–10 (10 being maximum). Gauge an "after" level of the issue's intensity, 0–10. You will likely

see your distress level decrease. As it does, the material that arises from one round (thoughts, feelings, glimpses of insights, memories, sensations) becomes what you focus on in the next round, and so on until your intensity level goes down to zero.

## A Round of Tapping consists of:

- The Setup Statement while tapping on the Side of the Hand (SH):
- Side of the Hand (SH) Take two fingers of your dominant hand and tap gently on your other hand, which is open, pinky side down. Tap on the fleshy part between the end of your pinky finger and wrist. (See diagram.)
- The Eyebrow Point (EB) At the beginning of the eyebrow, just above and to one side of the nose.
- Side of Eye (SE) On the bone bordering the outside corner of the eye.
- Under the Eye (UE)
  > On the bone just under either eye.
- Under the Nose (UN)
  > On the small area between the bottom of your nose and the top of your upper lip.
- Chin Point (CP)
  > The small space between your lower lip and your chin.
- Collarbone (CB)
  > The point one inch down and one inch over from either side of your collarbone (clavicle).

- Under the Arm (UA)
  - On either side of the body, about 4 inches below the armpit.
- Top of the Head (TH)
  - The area directly on the crown of the head.

In brief, **the Tapping Round consists of:**

- The Setup Statement
- Sequence with Reminder Phrases: Tapping on the following points:
  - SH (side of hand)
  - EB (eyebrow point)
  - SE (side of the eye)
  - UE (under the eye)
  - UN (under the nose)
  - CP (chin point)
  - CB (collarbone)
  - UA (under arm)
  - TH (top of head)
- Then take a releasing breath

CHAPTER 12

# Use the Technique of Tapping to Unmask Your Limitations and Access Your True Self

This section illustrates just how the tapping technique works with shadow qualities. Learn to use it to guide you gently, rapidly, and effectively toward the more hidden aspects of your personality, the very ones that may be keeping you stuck in your life *right now* without your conscious awareness.

Once these unseen qualities are identified, you will see how easy it is to pinpoint the powerful but inhibiting influence they have had over your thinking, and why. Tapping will assist you to look upon your masks with compassionate acknowledgment so that you can begin to unlock the gifts contained within each one.

A common mistake that is made when dealing with emotions is wanting to get rid of the "bad" ones the instant they arise. We fall into the trap of trying to either fix them or make them disappear. Furthermore, we judge ourselves harshly for having the unwanted feelings in the first place and then harbor shame and guilt for not being a more perfect person. This is a trap because instead of leading to release and relief, this approach leaves us in a perpetual cycle of blame, shame, and self-criticism. I think you will agree that if this were a useful way of handling our feelings, we all would have become unstuck by now. It seems to me, however, based on what my clients and others have said, many feel increasingly more downhearted from relying on this cycle, not less.

Shadow work is not new. Carl Jung's concept of the shadow, along with his other major contributions in the early to mid-1900s, gave the world an enduring way of understanding the self. A younger colleague of Sigmund Freud, Jung had a central concept called *individuation*—the lifelong process of figuring out the true self by decoding conscious and unconscious messaging. He believed that the shadow should never be ignored, that it contains natural, life-affirming, underdeveloped potentialities, along with its darker secrets. He also believed that unraveling the shadow's mysteries was a lengthy and laborious process that required a comprehensive analysis of the mind, dreams, and impulses, often taking many years, even decades, to complete. Many continue to carry his work forward, believing that coming to accept our shadow nature and assimilating it into our conscious personality is the foundation of good mental health. I wholeheartedly agree, and although this general framework is the one that most shapes my own work, who has decades to devote to feeling better?

The EFT tapping technique is uniquely suited for bringing the shadow to consciousness, much more quickly than traditional therapies. The breakneck-paced nature of our lives renders arduous, time consuming and expensive psychotherapy less relevant than it was only a short time ago.

Free association on the part of the patient—talking freely about whatever comes to mind for however long one wishes until "ready" to confront uncomfortable emotions, and the relative inactivity on the part of the therapist, silent nods, subtle encouragement and occasional interpretations—have given way to more pragmatic alternatives. Among these are short-term approaches, some of which are still based on traditional principles, but which see the therapist take on a more active, confrontational (confronting the defenses, not the person) stance instead of the supportive one used in long-term treatment.

Other methods bypass explorations of deep-seated emotions altogether and instead focus on the individual's thoughts, systematically challenging the validity of each one. Each of these theoretical frameworks, as well as many other "brief" forms of therapies, have evolved with research and refinements and have earned an invaluable place among treatment options that have been available over the past fifty years.

Mental health consumers, and likely anyone who feels as though he or she is drowning in fear however, would prefer to resolve their issues sooner rather than later. Those who suffer from more common problems—such as boarding an airplane, embarking on a first date, or wrestling with the incredibly perplexing fear of becoming too happy (or too financially successful, too independent, too decisive, too thin, or less cluttered) due to preexisting unworthiness—want to feel better as soon as they can. Therapists want the same for their patients whose suffering they are committed to easing.

As a result, the way in which many are going about getting help for their psychological wounds and emotional stumbling blocks is undeniably changing. Fewer people are willing or able to juggle therapy logistics on any regular basis. Carving out anywhere from one to two hours' worth of transportation for a 45-minute session, for example, is no longer practical for busy people. Current lifestyle trends have many looking to work through their issues in ways that are user and income-friendly while still helping them solve their real-life problems in tangible ways. Taking the scenic tour of one's emotional landscape over the course of many sessions has been replaced by more targeted, expedient, collaborative, and direct routes to a happier life.

## Faster Track to Solving Problems

You already know that tapping is a methodology that combines the principles of energy medicine, specifically acupuncture, with key components of cognitive psychology. You have read that as a mind/body technique, when aimed at the specific emotions, memories, events, or symptoms that block your productivity and peace of mind, it can bypass the thinking brain, circumventing stubborn and ingrained thoughts and beliefs that are difficult to undo with traditional therapies alone.

~

One of the most elegant features of EFT tapping is the deft way in which it approaches these resistant and so-called negative aspects of our thinking. First though, a word about *negativity*. I am often asked about the potential drawback or downside of looking at something we might deem *negative* for fear of giving it more weight, thereby accidentally reinforcing it. In my experience, the reverse is true. If the negative belief or emotion we are holding is not directly exposed, it will remain hidden and its influence will persist. Beyond this, our unconscious mind will reject and defeat any alternative ideas, new perspectives, or "positive" resolutions to our problem. No matter how many times we try to convince ourselves otherwise, our deeper belief wins out. We do not get what we want, necessarily. We get what we think we deserve. In short, we cannot outwit the negative energy in our thoughts, beliefs, or feelings. The negative component must be undone. Bringing all negativity and resistance out into the open where it can be acknowledged is the quickest and most powerful way to do this and offset its effects. Layering positive wishes on top of negative beliefs simply will not work to create the shifts we desire and in fact will only lead to feelings of frustration and failure.

A tremendous gift of personal power is available to us when we permit ourselves to honestly face our negative resistance such as fear, stubbornness, control, doubt, lack, limitation, avoidance, mistrust, and anything else that causes us to stay stuck. As mentioned earlier, stuck is less "can't" and more "won't." Personal acknowledgment of *all* our genuine emotions, no matter how ugly, weird, shameful, or illogical we think they are, is very much the seed of personal emotional competency. Our willingness to face our emotions honestly and fully sends a feedback loop to our most adult self that says we can handle our personal truth without needing to distort, alter or pretend it never happened.

The result is not something I would call positive thinking. It has nothing to do with looking on the bright side of things or seeing the glass as half-full. Instead, this level of self-realization is what cultivates an adult sense of mastery over oneself. There is no longer the compulsion to escape, to resort to the once lifesaving but childish coping tactic of "running outside to play" by means of excessive shopping, eating, drinking, drugging, posting, busying in order to shrink away from ourselves and our most uncomfortable truths. Facing these truths is how we stand in our factualness. It is how we stand firm *knowing what we know* about exactly what we have lived through, how we can take on reality and finally get real, how we can rise to our highest self, meet up with the wisdom already within and claim our wholeness. Stuckness is undone, ultimately, not by being perfect, but by being integrated.

## A Word About the Negative and Positive Sides of Who We Are

Because we possess both negative programming *and* positive potentialities at the same time, each of us is a combination of traits, *not one or the other*. The purpose behind shadow work is *integration*. By giving equal consideration to both our lower and higher qualities, our so-called negative and positive traits, we can incorporate these "parts" into a larger whole, a self that is *complete* rather than good or bad.

What follows are examples of how EFT tapping can be used to help you become a more authentic and confident person by lifting the masks of fear and defensiveness. They include brief vignettes and sample tapping dialogues. The clients are not actual clients of course; they are composite people drawn from years of experience working with EFT. They demonstrate how our self-concept affects our perception, feelings, and behavior. Go through them with this perspective in mind.

# A General Tapping Script for Feeling Stuck

Start here for the general problem of "feeling frustrated about feeling stuck."

## *Round #1*

**Setup Statement** (repeat 3 times to really help you focus in) while tapping on the Side of Hand (**SH**)

"Even though I feel stuck in my life right now, particularly in the area of (finances, relationship, health, productivity, other), and **I feel so frustrated**, *I deeply and completely accept myself anyway.*"

"Even though I feel stuck with (any of above) because things are not working out and **I feel so frustrated**, *I accept myself and how I feel.*"

"Even though **I feel so frustrated**, and I feel it in my (stomach, chest, throat, head, other), *I accept myself exactly where I am right now.*"

### Sequence with Reminder Phrases

**EB** "This frustration."

**SE** "This frustration about feeling stuck."

**UE** "This stomach frustration."

**UN** "This uncomfortable stomach frustration."

**CP** "I've felt this way for such a long time."

**CB** "I don't like this feeling."

**UA** It's really uncomfortable."

**TH** "I want to push this feeling away."

<u>Releasing Breath</u>

<u>Re-rate the Intensity</u>, 0–10 scale
Continue, using whatever thought, emotion or memory came to the surface as the *starting point* for the next round, round #2. For example:

**Setup Statement** (3 times) while tapping on the Side of Hand (**SH**)

"Even though I'm trying to push this feeling away right now because it's so uncomfortable, *I accept myself anyway.*"

**Sequence with Reminder Phrase**

EB "Pushing this frustration away."

SE "I'm pushing it away from me right now."

UE "I'm trying to get away from what I'm feeling in this moment."

UN "I can feel myself pushing the frustration deeper into my stomach."*

CP "I'm just trying to get more comfortable."

CB "No wonder my *stomach feels so awful."

UA "No wonder *I* feel so awful."

TH "Pushing my feelings away drives them further into my body.

*Wherever you feel the sensation in your body, i.e., chest, throat, temples, etc.

Releasing Breath

Re-rate the intensity, 0–10 scale
Continue, using whatever came up for you as the basis for the next round, round #3. For example:

**Setup Statement** (3 times) while tapping on the Side of Hand (**SH**)

"Even though I'm afraid I'll be overwhelmed by this feeling, *I accept myself anyway*.

**Sequence with Reminder Phrase:**

EB "I'm afraid to feel uncomfortable."

SE "I'm afraid I won't be able to handle it."

UE "I'm afraid the feeling will overwhelm me."

UN "So I push it down into my body."

CP "It's showing up as stomach issues."

CB "This is just information. Information about how I'm coping with my feelings.

UA "Just realizing that this is how I'm coping is a relief."

TH "What if I could learn to handle my emotions in a

way that actually helps me instead of making me feel worse?"

Releasing Breath

Re-rate the intensity, 0–10 scale
Continue with the next round, round 4:

**Setup Statement** (3 times) while tapping on the Side of Hand (**SH**)

"Even though I still have some remaining frustration, *it's okay to acknowledge it right now.*"

**Sequence with Reminder Phrase:**

EB "I feel okay acknowledging my emotion right now."

SE "My emotions are a part of me, and it feels good to be able to handle them."

UE "I'm feeling calmer in my body."

UN "This is a new sensation for me."

CP "I'm enjoying the calm feeling in my "stomach." *

CB "I'm noticing that I'm in the moment right now. I'm not running away from myself."

UA "I like this feeling of being present."

TH "I wonder how my life would change if I allowed myself to do this more often."

Releasing Breath

Re-rate the intensity, 0–10 scale

Having completed several rounds of tapping, repeat the problem statement out loud once again: "I feel so frustrated about feeling stuck," and measure how true the intensity feels right now on the 0–10-point scale. Notice whether the intensity of this specific emotion has come down. If it did not, that is perfectly fine. Continue with another round or two of tapping on the problem until it decreases, and your number is lower. Remember, you are paying attention to your discomfort instead of avoiding it, and you are allowing yourself to gradually process your emotion instead of suppressing it. This sends a calming signal to the stress center of the brain. You are beginning to switch off the flight, fight or freeze part of your brain and activate its relaxation response.

Then, do another round with positive words or images that *are true for you in* which you draw upon your experience in the previous rounds. No wishful thinking here. Go with what *you experienced*. The following is an example.

**Setup Statement** (3 times) while tapping on the Side of Hand (**SH**)

"Even though my frustration about feeling stuck has decreased, *I appreciate knowing I can make myself feel better.*"

**Sequence with Reminder Phrase:**

> EB "I see that I don't have to push my feeling of frustration away."

SE "I can acknowledge my feeling straight away."

UE "I don't have to drive my feelings into my body."

UN "I appreciate knowing what I feel."

CP "I accept myself even though I have been feeling stuck in my life."

CB "I love knowing what is going on with my emotions."

UA "I feel good understanding how I can make myself feel better."

ToH "I love knowing I have more influence than I thought over how I feel."

<u>Releasing Breath</u>

Repeat the original phrase and measure how true it feels now: "I feel so frustrated about being stuck in my life." 0–10

Look for signs that the intensity of your frustration either went down completely or another, deeper aspect of the issue has surfaced to be cleared. The beauty of tapping is that is distills issues down to the core so that they can be neutralized.

In the next chapter, you will find sample tapping dialogues that correspond to each of the masks described in Chapter 9. Use them as guidelines to see what is possible for you, as you look deeper within yourself, beneath your own mask. Feel free to substitute some of the wording to make the "script" more specific to you.

\ \ | / /
## CHAPTER 13
/ / | \ \

# Tapping Vignettes and Dialogue For Masks

## The Mask of People Pleaser Tapping Dialogue

Jacklyn, an elementary school teacher, was referred to me by her dentist because of stress-related teeth grinding and jaw clenching. She didn't see the need to consult a therapist, saying that her life was fine and she was "dealing with the same stress that everyone has," but she was willing to follow the recommendation of her dentist. History-taking revealed a pattern of always being available to everyone in her life with a tendency to put others' needs above her own. She rarely, if ever, says "no" to requests made of her time. Overwhelmed and often stretched thin, she has great difficulty setting boundaries and goes out of her way to make sure others are pleased with her. Jacklyn was unaware of this interpersonal pattern. In her view, she "just likes helping people and is happiest when she can make others happy." She is disconnected from the toll this pattern takes on her. She views her symptoms of teeth grinding and jaw clenching as medically based (her dentist does not) and thinks that taking a muscle relaxant may help.

Because Jacklyn was not consciously aware of her difficulty setting boundaries, I asked her to say the following statement out loud and then rate the intensity of its accuracy on a 0–10 scale: "It's okay to say 'no' when I don't want to do something." She immediately said, "It is definitely not okay to say 'no.'" and rated the intensity at a 10. "In fact," she said, "just picturing herself saying 'no' made her stomach drop." This reaction became the tapping target.

**Setup Statement**

"Even though the thought of saying 'no' makes my stomach drop, *I accept myself and how I feel.*"

"Even though saying 'no' makes me very uncomfortable and I feel it in my stomach, *I accept myself and how I feel.*"

"Even though I say 'yes' at times because I can't say 'no,' *I accept myself and how I feel.*"

EB "I'm too afraid to say 'no.'"

SE "I wouldn't think of it."

UE "I could never disappoint someone in that way."

CP "I couldn't stand it."

CB "It would make me too anxious."

UA "So I just say 'yes.'"

TH "I don't want the repercussions if I were to say what I want."

<u>Releasing Breath</u>

<u>Re-rate the intensity</u>, 0–10 scale
Jacklyn rated the intensity at a 7, saying that it was eye-opening to realize that she doesn't say "no" to anyone for a reason. She said she never looked at it in that way. We continued, simply using this new information as the start of the next sequence:

EB "I do what people ask of me without thinking of myself."

SE "I don't seem to ever think of what I need."

UE "I'm afraid they'll think I'm selfish."

UN "I've just always thought it was my responsibility to give the other person what they need."

CP "I guess I was happy making them happy"

CB "But was I really happy?"

UA "I'm not so sure now."

TH "I think I was just trying to avoid the consequences."

<u>Releasing Breath</u>

<u>Re-rate the intensity</u>, 0–10 scale
Jacklyn rated the intensity at a 5, saying that it felt good to connect the dots. She said the uncomfortable sensation in

her stomach was still there but much less. We continued with "the repercussions."

EB "I've always been worried about the repercussions."

SE "This must have something to do with my history."

UE "I felt I had to please everyone, especially my mom."

CP "I felt I had to please her, otherwise I'd be in trouble."

CB "She depended on me for a lot. I had to please her or else . . . I'd feel like I wasn't a good daughter."

UA "I guess I'm still living according to that old feeling."

TH "I had no idea I was still doing that!"

Releasing Breath

Re-rate the intensity, 0–10 scale

Jacklyn rated the intensity at a 3, saying that she would like to give herself the freedom to see whether it is always necessary to please others. This represents what is called a **cognitive shift**. Her thinking is beginning to change on its own simply by recognizing (and releasing) her deeper motivation. Until now, she had no conscious awareness that she was people-pleasing because of old programming that originated in her early relationship with her mother. The tapping allowed her to calm her body sufficiently so that she could quickly access her unconscious reasons for why she does what she does—often to the detriment of her emotional and physical health. We did one last tapping sequence:

EB "I'm beginning to think, *What about me?*"

SE "I want to make room for me, for my needs."

UE "I think I was frustrated and didn't even know it."

CP "I think it was showing up in my jaw as grinding and clenching."

CB "No wonder I felt so awful physically."

UA "My emotions were coming out in my sleep with teeth grinding."

TH "I don't want to hurt myself any longer. I'm open to the possibility of finding a better way of taking care of myself, a way that actually helps me."

<u>Releasing Breath</u>

Of course, Jacklyn has more work to do. But as is clear, the tapping helped her to recognize, rapidly and deeply, the old programming that has been running her without her conscious knowledge. With continued focus, tapping can continue to help reduce and even undo this pattern so that she can allow her real self to shine through. Instead of being ruled by the compulsive need to please, Jacklyn can finally find her authenticity, be fair to herself when it comes to meeting her needs as well as the needs of others, and proceed with a more balanced approach to life.

# The Mask of Victim Tapping Dialogue

Kiera, an administrative assistant for an executive in a major pharmaceutical company, came to see me because she was upset over an office situation in which she felt she was being ostracized by some of her coworkers. She said that she over-heard three of her coworkers referring to her as "needy and dramatic." History-taking revealed a pattern of interpersonal conflicts and severed friendships. The client said she often feels as though she is being used and taken advantage of, but when she needs something, "others never come through."

Kiera rated the intensity of "feeling used" at an 8. Because "feeling used" is not an emotion—it is an interpretation—I asked her how she felt toward her coworkers.

"Angry," she said. That became the tapping target.

## Setup Statement

"Even though things never go my way, no matter what I do, and **I feel angry** about that, *I accept myself and how I feel*."

"Even though I am baffled by how used I feel in my life, and **this makes me really angry**, *I accept myself and how I feel*."

"Even though I don't understand why bad luck and problems keep happening to me, and I honestly **feel so angry** and jealous of other, luckier people, *I accept myself and all my feelings*."

> EB "I feel angry at other people who seem to get all the breaks."

> SE "I feel so angry."

> UE "I feel so angry when I think about these other people."

> CP "I feel it in my body."

> CB "All this anger. It's like a knot in my stomach."

UA "These angry sensations in my body when I think about how unlucky I feel."

TH "I didn't know I had all this anger inside me."

Releasing Breath

Re-rate the intensity, 0–10 scale
Kiera rated the intensity still at an 8, saying that it felt satisfying to be saying out loud what she really feels. We continued.

EB "I don't know why such things keep happening to me."

SE "I wonder what's wrong with me."

UE "I must not deserve to have good things happen to me."

UN "That's it. Other people deserve good things more than I do.

CP "Others are more deserving."

CB "No wonder I feel so angry."

UA "What could be making me feel this way?"

TH "I think I've always felt this way."

Releasing Breath

Re-rate the intensity, 0–10 scale
I asked to tune into that last statement and notice how her body felt as she brought her attention to her words: "I think I've always felt this way." I asked her to allow her awareness

to drop into the feeling (s) associated with this statement and "listen" to what your body communicated to her. She said her body felt heavy, especially a heaviness in her chest along with a low feeling in her mind.

EB "My body feels heavy right now."

SE "This feeling of heaviness in my chest,"

UE "This low feeling in my mind and body."

UN "I know that I never let myself get this far with my feelings."

CP "The feeling is in my throat now. This lump in my throat."

CB "This lump is sadness. I'm feeling sadness at the thought that I don't feel deserving of attention or something like attention."

UA "I don't feel I deserve to have someone pay attention to me and what I need."

TH "I'm not sure I really matter as much as others do."

Releasing Breath

Re-rate the intensity, 0–10 scale
Kiera said that her anger had gone down to a 0, but a sadness came up quite strongly, an 8.

I asked Keira to whom did she not think she mattered? "My mother was always so busy. Her attention seemed to be everywhere else except on me. My younger brother was an athlete, a superstar, what you might call a golden boy. I remember times when I hoped he would break his leg or something so my mother would just be a normal mom. That is so terrible. Forget I even said that. I'm such a bad person for thinking that. Can I leave now?"

I suggested that we tap on the following:

EB "Mom gave him all the attention."

SE "He got it all."

UE "And I had those 'bad' thoughts."

UN "Such bad thoughts."

CP "I guess I wanted her attention too."

CB "But I couldn't ask her. I wouldn't dare. She was too busy. Too busy for me."

UA "There was that one time when I had strep throat. She took care of me. She stopped everything and paid attention to me. She rubbed my back and read to me. She did the same thing when I had a bad ear infection, too."

TH "She noticed me when I was sick. I see now that that was when she focused on me instead of my brother. I guess that's how I get my needs met, by always having a problem of some sort. This is starting to make sense."

Releasing Breath

As you can see, Kiera experienced a cognitive shift with these rounds of focused tapping. She began to connect her pattern of always being overwhelmed and helpless, hoping that others will bail her out of unfortunate situations and her history with her mother. She learned at an early age that while she couldn't ask or expect an appropriate measure of attention from her mother, she could get her to pay attention to her when she was sick. Young Kiera discovered the secret formula to getting what she needed—be sick or compromised or needy. This strategy, adaptive in childhood, became incorporated into her adult personality where it manifested as the overall persona of victim. Her *unconscious* patterns and the deep-seated, painful reasons for them started to become *conscious*. As awareness of her inner workings grew, her passivity and helpless attitude lessened. She has a deeper grasp of why she does what she does and a better understanding of her anger, sadness, guilt, and jealousy.

With continued tapping, I have every reason to believe that Kiera can let go of much of her victim nature as she faces her anger and sadness more directly. Where she has felt neglected by others for not meeting storehouse of unmet needs, she can now process her disappointment and put it into its proper perspective, the past. She can look forward to relating to others on equal footing with everyone else while no longer looking to other people to fill the void created by her personal history.

## Mask of "I'm fine" Tapping Dialogue

For the tapping to be effective on this mask, it must be aimed at a specific problem or issue with which the client is not in currently in touch. The challenge with this mask is that all problems are concealed by its sunshiney façade. Tapping on "I'm fine" per se without a more specific target is much too global and will not yield significant results.

Let's briefly meet Brooke, the social media sales consultant who came in to see me on the advice of her doctor. She has been suffering with migraine headaches (sudden onset, no known physical cause) for the past six months. She stays busy, going, going, going until she "crashes" at the end of the day. Her overall demeaner is bubbly and upbeat. As she shares her circumstance, she does so in a detached manner. Although she supplies details readily, she almost sounds as if she is talking about someone else. When I inquired about what was going on in her life approximately six months earlier, she described the following.

Brooke shared that she entered a new romantic relationship about eight or nine months ago. She said that she grew to care for her current boyfriend, Michael, early on and that the feelings were mutual. Despite completely opposite backgrounds, they are compatible in many ways and have common interests. They laugh, have meaningful talks, and enjoy one another's friends. At about the same time as her first migraine, however, their physical intimacy cooled off slightly. She said that that was her doing but she could not pinpoint the reason since she still felt very attracted to Michael.

Further inquiry revealed that Michael comes from a big, Italian family. He is one of five boys. They spent Christmas weekend at Michael's family home. She said she was warmly welcomed by everyone, particularly his mother. They gave her holiday gifts and did all they could to make her feel like a part of their family. It has been downhill ever since.

Brooke's family life was quite different. Her parents divorced bitterly when she, an only child, was six. She described some measure of emotional neglect as she spent most of her time with her father whom she described as a warm and caring man and much less time with her mother who had a problem with alcohol and other substances and suffered from what sounded like an untreated mood disorder. Her parents originally shared joint custody, but that arrangement was later amended by the court. By the time she was in middle school, Brooke was living with her dad. She maintained regular contact with her mother and continues to do so.

Back to Christmas. Brooke told me that when the weekend was over and she was back in her apartment, she broke down sobbing. As is her pattern, she dismissed her intense emotional reaction as a "crying jag" and didn't look back. In fact, the more she spoke about the details, the more she alternated between smiling and fidgeting and sounding rather matter of fact. At other moments as we turned to other aspects of her life, she appeared curiously cheerful and lighthearted. Clearly, her nonverbal expressions did not match the content she was revealing.

The timing of symptom onset is a crucial factor when determining the root cause of a problem and invariably provides important clues. The headaches and her subtle sexual withdrawal seem to coincide with the Christmas weekend.

The tapping part of our session centered on the weekend, Michael's mother, and Brooke's intense sobbing. I asked her to focus on her recollection of the holiday and to tell me what part of the weekend stands out. She said that what stood out for her was the warmth in her boyfriend's home. I asked her to describe how she feels about the warmth when she thinks about it now. She began to smile at the exact moment her eyes welled up with tears. She attempted to change the subject. Using only the information she provided, I led her through the following tapping sequence after I asked her to rate intensity of how disturbing the weekend feels to her now. She gave her overall upsetting feeling a 9.

**Setup Statement**

"Even though I don't want to look at my reaction to the warmth that weekend, *I choose to accept myself, anyway*."

"Even though I don't even want to think about how warmly I was treated by Michael's mother that weekend, *I choose to accept myself, anyway*."

"Even though it makes me really uncomfortable in my body to remember all that warmth, *I choose to accept myself, anyway*."

EB "There's something about that warmth."

SE "Something about all that warmth for me."

UE "Thinking about it right now is making me queasy in my stomach."

UN "This queasiness in my stomach."

CP "This 'warmth' queasiness in my stomach."

CB "This reaction in my body to the warmth that was shown to me."

UA "I don't know what to do with it."

TH "I never experienced it before."

<u>Releasing Breath</u>

<u>Re-rating the intensity</u> on the 0–10 scale, she gave it a 5, down from a 9.

We continued to the next round, picking up from where we left off.

EB "I have never experienced that much warmth before."

SE "Something about it almost made me feel sick."

UE "I felt almost sick about the warmth."

UN "I wonder what it is about me and warmth that is causing this reaction in my body."

CP "I'm not used to it. I never had it."

Crying now. She was unable to speak but she continued to tap through the points while I verbalized for her based on the whole picture she provided.

CB "It hurt when Michael's mother was so nice to me when my own mother wasn't."

Crying more deeply.

UA "I've been in a lot of pain about going without warmth for so long."

TH "And I didn't realize it until now."

<u>Releasing Breath</u>

<u>Re-rated her intensity</u>
Her crying gradually stopped, and she offered her intensity measurement without my asking. It was a 3.

My objective in describing this tapping sequence with Brooke is to illustrate how rapidly this technique can find the opening for emotional release. Brooke obviously has more work to do as she processes her feelings about her relationship with her mother. A few minutes of tapping is not going to resolve years of buried emotions. What is striking here, however, is that it is not her emotional pain that is causing her symptoms. Rather it is the suppression of them. This short course of EFT loosened her defense mechanism of detachment, which showed up as the casual refrain of "I'm fine" whenever her painful feelings surfaced. The fact of the matter is that Brooke is not "fine." She has many strengths but underneath them she hides feelings of powerlessness, rage, sadness, and longing. The more she can open to these feelings and face her painful but authentic truth, the less she will have to pretend that they do not exist. She will have the opportunity to live a more integrated and wholistic life, not merely existing in a false state of "fineness."

# The Mask of Apologizer Tapping Dialogue

Christopher, a dance school instructor, came in for a consultation because of vague feelings of "being down" and a general lack of productivity. During the course of history taking, he demonstrated a personality style characterized by tentativeness, caution and nervousness. As he entered my office, he apologized for taking up my time. This caught my attention as did the additional apologies that followed.

His presenting problem centered around his recent dating experiences which were unsuccessful. He said that the feedback he's received from the men he's gone out with two or three times was some version of "doesn't bring enough to the table," "Is too passive" and "doesn't share much about himself." When asked how he felt about this, he answered with, "It hurts but it's true. I *am* like that; I am afraid that I will burden others. I don't want anyone to feel sorry for me." The conversation focused on what happens internally when he thinks about opening up in a relationship. I didn't have him measure any intensity until we landed on a more specific target. We began with some general tapping.

## Setup Statement

"Even though I feel like I'm burdening others if I open up and show myself, *I am willing to accept myself, anyway.*"

"Even though I don't want others to feel obligated to listen to me, *I am willing to accept myself, anyway.*"

"Even though I have a tendency to feel wrong if I focus on myself, *I am willing to accept myself, anyway.*"

EB "I'm afraid I'll be a burden."

SE "I'm afraid I *am* a burden."

UE "Am I doing this right? The Tapping? I'm sorry if I'm not."

UN "I feel so tentative all the time.

CP "I feel as though I have to always be so careful. I walk on eggshells."

CB "It's hard for me to ask for what I need or want."

UA "I constantly worry about what others think."

TH "I feel everything is my fault."

<u>Releasing Breath</u>

<u>Re-rate intensity</u>, 0–10 scale

Christopher rated his intensity with a 7, saying that the truth of this rang strongly for him. He immediately said that he felt some sadness as he thought about how much he keeps himself in check, how afraid he is about making mistakes. We continued.

EB "I'm afraid to make a mistake."

SE "I'm afraid my mistakes will make things worse."

UE "I can't deal with anyone being angry with me."

UN "I can't make mistakes."

CP "I just can't."

CB "I have to stay in my box."

UA "It doesn't feel right to go outside of my box."

TH "I have to know my place and I'm worried about stepping outside."

<u>Releasing Breath</u>

<u>Re-rate intensity</u>, 0–10 scale

Christopher rated his intensity at a 6, a slight decrease from a high of 8.

At this point I introduced the following question to see if there is a buried memory that is linked to his character traits of passivity and over responsibility. I'm interested in seeing whether the memory of a past event could be blocking his spontaneity and interpersonal fluency.

*"When was the first time you realized that it wasn't safe to make a mistake?"*

Christopher immediately went to the following memory: The time when I was seven and my parents were having an argument. I thought I could stop them from yelling at one another by making chocolate milk for the three of us. Well, I knocked the entire jug of milk onto the floor which made them angrier, especially my father. He started yelling at my mom and blamed her for what I did. The next thing I remember is him storming out of the house. My mom was crying as she cleaned up the mess. I tried to help but I think she said that I was just in the way, that I'd make things worse. I can't be sure if she actually said that but that's the way that I felt.

*We resumed the Tapping, focusing on this important memory and his feelings associated with it. I specifically wondered that if he could go back and express his feelings to his mother, what would he say or do?*

EB "I'm sorry, Mom."

SE "I'm so sorry that I upset you."

UE "I didn't mean to make things worse."

UN "I was only trying to help."

(Tearing up)

CP "I tried to help, and I made things worse."

CB "I felt so responsible for what happened."

UA "It was all my fault."

TH "No wonder I'm so afraid to initiate anything. It's starting to make sense now."

Releasing Breath

Christopher rated the intensity of the target memory of "spilled milk" at 0, saying it is essentially a "non-issue." The tapping thus far was successful in removing the unconscious block between his current behavior and the event which created it. Although he has more work to do in this area, he is much less likely to find refuge in his present behavior pattern of passivity since he was able to connect his feelings to the source, namely his mother. The need for him to unconsciously displace his apology onto everyone has decreased substantially. He has taken the first and most important step toward self-awareness and authenticity.

## The Mask of Over-Competence Tapping Dialogue

Grace, a real estate agent who owns her own company, sought help for issues related to overwhelm, stress, and emotional overeating. The issue that prompted her visit centered around her complaint that she "has to do it all" in both her personal and professional life. She said that she feels resentful that she "must keep all the balls up in the air herself since no one else, including her spouse, is intellectually equipped to handle things as well as she. Several times during our initial conversation, she referred to significant people in her life as either "too dumb or too incompetent" to be relied on.

She was already familiar with EFT. After taking a history, I went straight to what I thought was the heart of her distress. I asked her to say the words "It's not safe to rely on anyone," out loud and to rate the degree of resonance this statement has for her. She measured the truthfulness at a 10 on the 0–10 scale. We began the tapping:

**Setup Statement**

"Even though I feel as though I can't depend on anyone, *I accept myself and how I feel.*"

"Even though I *know* I can't depend on anyone, *I accept myself and all of my feelings.*"

"Even though I probably have my reasons for not depending on anyone, *I deeply accept myself.*"

EB "It's not smart to rely on others."

SE "It never goes well."

UE "It would be disappointing to count on someone other than myself."

UN "People just can't keep up with me. That's a fact."

CP "I have to handle it all. Who else would or could if I didn't?"

CB "I can't let myself count on anyone. I'll just be let down."

UA "I *won't* let myself count on anyone."

TH "I take care of everything because it's safer that way."

Releasing Breath

Re-rate intensity, 0–10 scale
Grace measured her belief at a 10. It did not move at all with this round of tapping. We continued.

EB "There's no way I'm ever going to rely on anyone for anything."

SE "I will never put myself in that position."

UE "It's not smart to put myself in that position, again."

UN "I'm tired of doing everything but I have to."

CP "I must have my reasons for such a strong position."

CB "I'm not going to ever change this."

UA "I don't have to change this."

TH "No one can make me change this."

Releasing Breath

<u>Re-rate the intensity</u>, 0–10 scale

The intensity didn't move. She was still at a 10, however, she appeared to be more curious about the strength of her own conviction.

> EB "This must have to do with my history."
>
> SE "I certainly couldn't rely on my mother and it was just the two of us."
>
> UE "She was too self-absorbed and needy."
>
> UN "I was actually smarted than her."
>
> CP "That was a good thing."
>
> CB "If I wasn't, we'd both be in trouble."
>
> UA "I had to keep things afloat, even as a little girl."
>
> TH "If I didn't manage things, I don't know what would have happened to us."
>
> <u>Releasing Breath</u>

<u>Re-rate intensity</u>, 0–10 scale

Intensity dropped to a 6. This decrease does not mean that Grace is prepared to give up her persona of always being in charge and the smartest one in the room. It does reflect an increase in her awareness that there may be a connection between her persona and the need to take care of herself at a young age since her mother could not. Instead of seeing her beliefs as airtight and a function of *who she is*, she can perhaps view them as *what they are*—crucial survival mechanisms that helped her deal with an emotionally threatening childhood situation.

Grace has taken an important step toward understanding and gradually dismantling her defensive armor. Holding onto it and keeping it intact as it is will only serve to keep her stuck, overwhelmed, and in a state of resentment.

## The Mask of Avoidance

Collin, a successful small business owner, sought EFT for "stress in his relationship" which, as was soon revealed, is tied to his difficulty saying "no." He attributes this to his extreme discomfort with confrontation. The specific event that prompted his visit with me had to do with a fight between him and his fiancée. Although he knew what he wanted to say to her "to defend himself," he felt utterly paralyzed to do so. Instead, he shut down, as is his pattern, and withdrew into silence for the entire Valentine's Day weekend they spent at an island resort. When we met, he said he felt depressed, disillusioned, and concerned about the future of his relationship.

After obtaining a history, I asked him to tell me the story of exactly what happened, especially right before he noticed himself shutting down. *Tell the Story* is one of the tapping techniques designed to isolate the triggering event. Much the way individual frames make up a film sequence, Tell the Story proceeds, step by step, frame by frame, until a point is reached in the story that feels uncomfortable. The frame with the most emotion becomes the tapping target.

Here, the client takes us to a point in the argument where he could feel himself shutting down and "checking out" as he sensed a confrontation was building. I asked him to consider the statement "I'm afraid of confrontation" and to rate the intensity of the fear. He rated it as an 8 on the 0-10 scale.

**Setup Statement**

"Even though I felt that a confrontation was coming, and I didn't know how to handle it, *I accept myself and how I feel.*"

"Even though I felt her coming at me verbally and wanted her to stop, I just froze instead, *I accept myself and how I feel.*"

"Even though I just wanted to remove myself, and I did so mentally, *I accept myself and how I feel.*"

> EB "She was raising her voice."
>
> SE "She was raising her voice at me and it made me so uncomfortable."
>
> UE "I felt so uncomfortable in my body."
>
> UN "I just wanted to run away."
>
> CP "I hated that moment. I can feel that discomfort in my body right now, especially in my chest and throat, as I think about what happened."
>
> CB "I just needed to escape but had nowhere to go."
>
> UA "This awful confrontation feeling in my chest and throat."
>
> TH "No wonder I just want to get away."
>
> Releasing Breath

Rate intensity, 0–10 scale
Collin measured the discomfort in his body at an increased intensity level of 8 to 9. I made him a bit more comfortable before continuing by doing a quick round of tapping on

"These are just my feelings. I am okay where I am. It is safe where I am right now." We continued as soon as he felt ready to get back into it. I asked him to signal when he was comfortable enough to resume.

"Even though a part of me wanted to run away in that moment, a bigger part of me wants to be able to stay and defend myself."

(Note the slight shift in attitude. He moved from total avoidance to partial avoidance. Things are going in the right direction.)

EB "I want to speak up for myself."

SE "I want to tell her how I feel."

UE "It's so hard for me but I don't know why."

UN "I feel like a deer in headlights."

CP "This deer in headlights freezing feeling."

CB "Something stops me."

UA "The only way I can protect myself in that moment is by completely shutting down. That only seems to make her angrier and *that* makes me run all the faster!"

TH "What if I could learn another way to protect myself that helps me rather than keeps me stuck?"

Releasing Breath

Rate intensity, 0–10 scale
He measured the intensity of *needing to escape* at a 3, down from an 8–9 only a few minutes before. As he began to see his

shutting down as a defense mechanism—a solution of sorts rather than the way he *is*—he could consider other alternative ways of responding. He said this gives him a feeling of hope. We continued.

EB "I'm not used to speaking up for myself."

SE "I never could as a kid."

UE "My mother would fly off into rages. We never knew when this was coming."

UN "I learned to just stay out of her way as much as possible."

CP "When she would start to yell and scream, I would hide out in my room."

CB "I would wait her out. That was all I could do, or else . . ."

UA "Or else . . . she might escalate, and I couldn't take that chance. My sister and I were home alone with her, since my father worked a lot."

TH "Hiding was my only choice. What else could I do?"

<u>Releasing Breath</u>

<u>Rate intensity</u>, 0–10 scale
Collin's level of discomfort dropped to a 2 as he could now see that his "hiding" was a survival mechanism, the only way his young self knew to cope with a threatening situation. He softened as his eyes became moist.

EB "I feel for that kid."

SE "He was just doing his best."

UE "He . . . I . . . was all alone."

UN "I had to figure out how to duck all on my own."

CP "Those were rough years."

CB "I wish I had help to figure things out, but I didn't back then."

UA "I guess this is why it's so hard for me to let someone know how I really feel. I always had to just go it alone."

TH "I've been handling things that same way ever since. I have a few things to learn in this department. And I want to learn them."

Releasing Breath

Of course, this is just the beginning for Collin. Instead of feeling constrained by insecurity and stuck in understandable but outdated ways of coping with his fear, he has discovered that other, more constructive, and powerful ways of defending himself are within reach. He touched on his capacity for self-compassion in recognizing that his younger self was alone. This will allow him to bring a level of depth, tenderness, and flexibility to his otherwise rigid and avoidant persona.

# The Mask of Rescuer and Fixer Tapping Dialogue

Terry, a radiology technician, was referred on the advice of her health care professional who saw her for a routine medical exam. The results indicated that Terry, in her early forties, has hypertension and suffers from insomnia. The doctor thought that Terry could benefit from EFT for both symptom relief and ongoing stress management.

Terry Googled EFT before coming in. She was skeptical but so in need of a good night's sleep that she was willing to try almost anything. She denied the existence of any additional problems.

History taking revealed a woman who is the sole caretaker of her mother who has early onset Alzheimer's. Her father died when she was eleven. She has two younger siblings, both of whom live out of state. Terry works full time at a large teaching hospital, sits on the board of a non-profit and volunteers at a pet shelter every other week. She can often be found preparing and delivering nutritious meals to her elderly neighbors and looks in on them daily. She shared with pride that she has not taken a day off from work in almost three years. Although she has the financial means, she has not taken a vacation or spent any time away from her responsibilities during that time. When she does have holidays and long weekends off, she either offers to work for coworkers so they can enjoy days off with their families or she puts in time at her volunteer position. When I inquired into her self-care, she told me that she "doesn't do self-care." We started there.

I asked Terry to complete the following sentence out loud: "If I took better care of myself, I . . ." She immediately answered with "I would feel too uncomfortable." And measured the truthful resonance of that at a 9 on the 0–10 scale.

## Setup Statement

"Even though I don't do self-care because it makes me too uncomfortable, *I accept this truth about myself.*"

"Even Though I don't *want* to take care of myself because something about it makes me too uncomfortable, *I accept myself and how I feel.*"

"Even though I guess I neglect myself in some way, *I accept where I am right now.*"

EB "Taking time for myself makes me uneasy."

SE "This uneasiness about taking time for myself."

UE "I don't do it. I don't take care of myself."

UN "For some reason, I treat *myself* differently than I treat others."

CP "That's the truth."

CB "I seem to put everyone else's needs ahead of my own."

UA "I'm not even on my own self-care list."

TH "I wonder what makes me uncomfortable about taking care of myself."

<u>Releasing Breath</u>

Re-rate intensity, 0–10 scale
Terry measured the accuracy of the statement "I feel too uncomfortable taking care of myself," at a 9, with no change from her initial measurement. I then suggested that she say the following statement out loud: "I don't deserve the time and attention." She begins to tear up.

> EB "Somewhere inside me, I feel like I don't deserve attention."
>
> SE "I don't deserve attention."
>
> UE "I don't deserve it."
>
> (Shaking her head emphatically)
>
> UN "That's it. I'm not worthy of it."
>
> CP "No wonder I reject it."
>
> CB "It feels wrong to focus on *me*."
>
> UA "And just better to focus on everybody else."
>
> (Deep sigh. Shoulders relaxing)
>
> TH "I just realized something about myself. I just figured out that I don't feel like I have the right to take time out for myself."
>
> (Sitting up taller, nodding)
>
> Releasing Breath

Rate intensity, 0–10 scale
I asked her to go back and test for intensity by repeating the statement "I don't deserve the time and attention." She said

although that is still true, she wonders why she feels that way. A subtle but meaningful cognitive shift has occurred. She has moved one step away from *identifying with her belief* to *questioning her belief.* It cannot be stressed enough that without this dis-identification with the belief, the persona cannot change because it has no objectivity with which to see itself.

This is merely the beginning for Terry. She must investigate what in her history explains her feelings of unworthiness. Tapping can rapidly help her to go deeper into the origin of her beliefs about where her self-value comes from. At the present time, she obviously derives a sense of self-worth from feeling needed. As you can no doubt see, she has a self-worth void and is trying to fill it by over-doing for others in and it is greatly contributing, if not causing, her physical symptoms. With continued Tapping, I feel strongly that Terry can look forward to healing her belief that she is undeserving and can treat herself with the kindness, warmth, and compassion she affords others.

## CHAPTER 14

# Getting Unstuck: A New Identity

I began this book by asserting that coming to know our truest self is perhaps the single-most important step we can take toward steering our own course in life and taking possession of its direction and meaning. The approach I offer to finding our authenticity, and by extension a path to an empowered life, rests on the premise that human beings—every human being—has a right to self-determination, the process by which a person has the ability to manage and control his or her own life.

Each of us is an autonomous being, not an appendage of another. Just as none of us belongs to anyone, neither does anyone belong to us; each of us has the right to exist for our own sake, according to our own well-thought-out convictions, values, and innate guidance. As we have seen from the people we have just met, far too many of us are guided by an almost opposite sense.

During our young lives, many factors affect and shape who we become. Family dynamics and societal and environmental forces all play a crucial part. Nowhere is the influence on a child's maturation more evident however, than in the way her parents (or caretakers) respond to the fulfillment of her emotional needs. Those of us whose parents or their proxies unwittingly conveyed that we had to repress all or some of our needs, in order to please, protect, soothe, or sustain them, may have absorbed the message that the purpose of our existence is to satisfy the needs of others, others who themselves had to satisfy someone's else's needs before them.

Such is human nature and often the effect of conditional love—not necessarily bad or wrong, simply a human characteristic. As we noticed in the case vignettes, the deeper identities of the individuals we met were hidden beneath more visible ones, the very same they developed in order to meet the demands and expectations of those whose love and acceptance they needed most. We can see that the price paid for this is steep and long-ranging and shows up in all manner of everyday interactions. Trying to succeed in life without having developed enough self-regard is to live feeling like an imposter anxiously waiting to be found out. Then, when we don't succeed, by virtue of feeling like an undeserving fraud or because our emotional battery is drained, we end up blaming ourselves. In some cases, we feel too guilty to even permit ourselves the opportunity to dream, or hope, or expect good things. We get what we think we deserve, remember? Not what we want.

One of the most difficult truths we must realize about ourselves is how wrong we have been about so many things. Not about how imperfectly we may have done things, or not done them. Rather how afraid we were to admit that those on whom we depended most were wrong about us. When our newly divorced mother dressed up and went on dates, for example, leaving us home alone to care for our younger siblings, the explanation we gave to our ten-year-old self was that we were simply not worth staying home for. We must now come to see and know that it was she who failed us. If our father asked us to keep evidence of his affair a secret from our mother, and we did for fear that our world would unravel if we didn't, now is the time to confront our own feelings of having been let down by the very giant in whose care we had hoped to find a safe place. And when our baby sister was diagnosed with a serious illness requiring extensive and protracted medical treatment and she received the lion's share of our parents' attention, we internalized our feelings and felt rageful and frustrated inside, and guilty. It wasn't safe to let out these feelings, and we didn't think we would have been heard anyway. It was easy to feel second-rate and undeserving. No wonder we feel as adults that money shouldn't come to us, or love or even happiness itself. Even if we were to have any one of these, we're fearful (and convinced) it won't last. The logical conclusion: don't bother to expect good things because we will just end up disappointed.

To admit that our parents were not only wrong, they were wrong about us, can be destabilizing, even threatening. Conceding to their flaws without rationalizing their flaws away can not only arouse painful feelings in us, doing so can stir guilt-laden feelings of disloyalty. On some level we know that their best efforts were sincere; they did their best. But the difficult truth, the one that we turn away from and defend against vehemently, is that their best was woefully inadequate. This is not to indict anyone. It is to simply say that you did not receive what you needed, regardless of the reason, and the reason was not your fault. Allowing the humanness of our parents to enter the consciousness of our young minds would have been extremely overwhelming and terrifying. Children cannot mitigate the effects of being left alone or emotionally abandoned. That would be just too much to bear. A child invents ways with which to adapt and survive their parents' misguidedness.

## Compassionate Recognition

Most of us walk around with a huge but invisible load of blameworthiness on our shoulders. We feel guilty for not measuring up to an ideal image of ourselves, ashamed of the desperate things we've done to win love and approval and bewildered by the manner in which we have tried to get the outer world to meet our needs. We harbor self-reproach about the choices we have made from jealousy, comparison, inadequacy, revenge, or impulsivity. We regret our excesses, overindulgences, and irresponsible behavior. Although we sense all this about ourselves, most of us sweep it aside, push the guilt and self-judgment deep down into some emotional vault, and proceed through life as if none of this matters. We resolve to polish our carefully crafted facades, deceiving ourselves and others into thinking we're "fine." This is not an action plan for personal health and success. By contrast, it is a formula for self-estrangement and the subtle (or not-so-subtle) building of an emotional wall that keeps us from true intimacy and authentic connection. As discussed in an earlier chapter, we cannot love anyone until we love ourselves. *The other side of the coin is equally true: if we do not feel lovable, it will be very difficult to trust that anyone else loves us.* Our belief that anyone can love and accept us stops at the point at which we doubt that we are worthy of love. Even if we attempt to talk ourselves out of feeling unlovable, the deeper belief prevails, and we inadvertently push the potential of love away. We sabotage the very thing we crave the most.

By looking at ourselves through a lens of compassion, we have the chance to understand why we took the actions that we took or didn't take. We can bring insight to why certain relationships may have failed, why we lost an opportunity or the reason we avoided one. We can inquire into why we broke a sacred promise to someone. Compassionate recognition does not let us off the hook from reality. It will not have us seeing as right what was wrong. Instead, it has us looking into the context within which the action was taken. It asks us for our *because*. When beating ourselves up for a wrongdoing we feel we have committed, we owe it to ourselves to honestly and undefendedly answer the why and pinpoint the internal, unvarnished considerations that led to the behavior. Even the most confounding, egregious, or offensive actions make sense in some context. Think back to our traveler to the Grand Canyon who ran away from the vista and toward what she perceived was a safer place. Context.

## Accepting Your Own Apology

So many people are waiting, yearning, to receive a sincere apology from whomever hurt, wronged, or disappointed them. And in many of my clients' cases, I think they are owed one. Yet waiting for an acknowledgment or expression of remorse could be an endless wait. Perhaps the person who hurt you is too stubborn, too unaware, too proud, or too self-absorbed to ever offer up a heartfelt apology. Perhaps he or she is no longer living. Too often I have seen people more invested in extracting an apology from someone not likely to give it than they are with getting on with their lives. Even the grave is not too far for some, as they hold onto the unrelenting wish that someone who has died can still make up for past hurts.

It is not easy to let go of the wish to level the playing field when we feel we have been wronged, to feel as though we have power equal to whomever deeply upset us. When we feel injured, abandoned, betrayed, or neglected, being on the receiving end of unfairness or aggression makes us feel small and powerless. While it is natural to want to be on equal emotional footing with whomever has injured us, my clients prove that waiting indefinitely for this to happen is one of the most unavailing investments we can make. Waiting for an unlikely apology to come our way can cost us in immeasurable ways. Putting so much time and energy into the hollow endeavor of expecting what cannot, or will not, be given is an exercise in futility. To ease the disappointment and heartache to which we ourselves have been unknowing contributors, perhaps the most viable apology we can accept is the one from ourselves to ourselves. Only by acknowledging our participation in a negative cycle can we have any hope of breaking it.

## Forgiveness. Yes, Forgiveness

I find that few people are enthused about forgiveness. Receiving it, maybe. Offering it? Not so much. While we might like the idea of forgiving (it sounds so noble), it can conjure up images that are incompatible with our sense of righteousness, fair-mindedness, and reasonableness. It can reduce our thinking to a reluctant acceptance that whatever was done to hurt us wasn't so bad and neither was the person who did the wounding. It can leave us feeling that "they" have gotten away with something utterly unfair while we're consumed with revenge fantasies, imaginary comebacks, and the ticking away of lost time and missed opportunities as we replay the injury in our heads. It can drain the adrenaline from our bodies, robbing it of what one of my very first clients, a woman in her late eighties used to say, the "piss and vinegar" that pumps you up, when what you really feel is deflated at the hands of someone who hurt you. When you are on the receiving end of someone's bad mood, bad day, or bad twenty years, feeling small and helpless is rough. The sense of powerlessness and impotence is almost unbearable.

We can all agree that nowhere is this truer in everyday living than in childhood where little ones are literally trapped by circumstances; held hostage by grownups who control virtually everything. If raised in a particularly abusive or neglectful home in which they could not speak out against frightening, controlling or emotionally neglectful adults, children grow up with an internal sense of powerlessness that robs them of their spirit, their strength and a sense of control and hope.

Powerlessness, like any strong emotional current, needs a place to land, a psychological home to settle into. If it does not find cover in a personality that is passive, emotionally flat, or anxious, it can flip on itself, whisking what was once legitimate victimization into a subtle, lifelong froth of resentment and indignation. Afterall, when one is trying not to nosedive into sadness and disappointment, nothing quite keeps you aloft like the energy of feeling wronged. It is rocket fuel to the wounded ego. To compensate for feeling defenseless as children, we become overly defended as adults, finally gaining what feels like the long-awaited upper hand in life. By withholding forgiveness from whomever has wronged us, we can feel strong, important and in control. Refusing to let go of grievances can make us feel covertly superior, holding another's relief in our hands, as we no doubt felt someone once held ours. This self-generated mood elevator, our mind's way of shifting the balance of power from "them" to us, is something we do not let go of easily.

I've always thought it a useful question, "Is it better to be right or happy?"

How many of us through our actions answer, "It's better to be right."?

I think we hold onto a belief that if we can convince the wrongdoers that we're right and they've been wrong all along, we'll have gotten through to them and that alone will make us both right and happy in the end. The kind of "happy" that comes from feeling vindicated, validated, and understood for our pain. The kind of "happy" that says "You finally see me. You see how you have hurt me. You see how you have neglected me. You see how you have abandoned me. "Now, with your acknowledgment (and apology), I can finally move on. I am finally worth something."

This is one of the most powerful and enduring daydreams of our lives. The hope that this day will come lives on, no matter our age, evidence to the contrary, whether we have seen the person in decades, or even whether he or she is still alive. Such is the unrelenting wish to be loved and adequately cared for by those whose love we craved and counted on. It is a hope that dies hard on its own, if at all. In fact, the longer our pleas go unheard the more we seem to continue to beg.

Forgiveness is a radical act, an about-face in our thinking.

It is radical because, by definition, it is an acceptance of the way things and people are—a sharp departure from our typical way of thinking. To forgive is to drop the pretense that the past can be rewritten. To forgive is to let go of the fantasy that people will stop disappointing us. To forgive is to surrender to the fact that what happened in the past really happened and not gloss over it with denial or haze. Mostly, forgiveness is a willingness to stop waiting around for our history to change or for certain people to apologize for it.

It is a radical act to respect the reality of our past, and even more radical to forgive ourselves for mistakes made while trying to escape it. Before we can forgive however, we must name what it is that we are forgiving. When it comes to forgiving others, we must be willing to recall what was done to us, to lean into the pain or discomfort that we have been avoiding all our lives. (Did I say forgiveness was radical?) In order to grow beyond our pain, we must first feel it.

Oftentimes, a new client will describe the details of a very dysfunctional early home life. He or she will go into detail about the horrendous things they experienced. Then when asked how they feel about what happened to them, they say, "I know my parents did the best they could."

When asked to describe their own emotions, they are at a loss. They are completely out of touch with their feelings about what took place; they are detached from their emotional reactions toward their parents or caregivers. Most strikingly, they are disconnected from their essential vulnerability, from their own basic emotional needs. In fact, they detest the mere mention of it. They hurry to forgive those who have disappointed them before visiting upon the very disappointment that lives within. By skipping over their own pain, many of my clients tell themselves they are "okay," that they are not hurting.

Interestingly, these clients often suffer from the signs and symptoms associated with carrying unresolved grief and unprocessed anger. They may have "forgiven" in their thoughts but not in their hearts. Their heads tell them they have let go of resentments, bitterness, blame, and pain, but their energy and behavior say otherwise. They may *want* to forgive, but they don't know how.

We cannot talk ourselves into forgiveness. The most important thing to know about this kind of grace is that it cannot occur without first feeling the effects of what was experienced. We don't heal by blocking or burying our pain but by talking about it, by letting it out. And by letting it "out," I mean sharing it with another human being. Because our deepest wounds are created by and within human relationships, it takes another human relationship to heal them. From a place of truthful, conscious reality one can choose to move beyond previously unacknowledged pain. By doing this, one honors the self while moving toward forgiveness of another. It is not an either/or approach. It is not, "I forgive you while denying my own feelings." It is, "I know what I feel. I feel what I feel. Feeling my disappointment, pain, sadness, anger at what was done to me, I choose to be okay, anyway. I choose to see myself as worthy, deserving and enough, even if you didn't."

From an emotionally sober place within, when we choose to see the flaws and limitations in others rather than overly react to them or feel responsible for them, we can begin to establish our own identity. No longer dependent on their approval, we step into a more autonomous, self-governed, and self-defined existence.

Forgiveness cannot (and should not) be forced or pinned down. If we cannot forgive ourselves, it is a forgiving gesture to compassionately acknowledge that we have done things that were hurtful to ourselves and others while we were awkwardly finding our way. Where we can, and if appropriate, making amends is a move toward self-respect as well as a move to respect whomever we offended or hurt. By seeking to deeply understand why we have done the things we've done, we give ourselves the opportunity to see ourselves in context, to grapple with our feelings of anger, disappointment and shame.

Taking a step back and viewing our past actions empathically helps us to unpack our motivations. Almost without exception, when my clients choose to treat themselves in this way, they learn a great deal about their inner life and begin to cultivate a better, more realistic, and adult relationship with themselves. An interesting thing happens when we see ourselves from a perspective that is more self-aware, even-handed, and insightful: we do not become sloppy, reckless individuals who let ourselves off the accountability hook easily or casually. On the contrary, we step into a more psychologically mature self and show up for our own lives and the world with greater clarity, discernment, and groundedness. We have a lighter touch and a deeper capacity. In essence, we become more like the adults we yearned for a lifetime ago, only this time we are the beneficiary of our own championing.

~

*Yes, but . . . do they deserve my forgiveness?*, you may be shouting in your head.

The best answer I have come up with for this often-asked question is they deserve it as much as you do. If you think you deserve forgiveness, keep in mind that others feel the same way.

For some reason in the human condition, especially when it comes to relationships, we have a much easier time pardoning our own missteps and infractions than we do those of another. However, whether they (and you) *deserve* to be forgiven is the least-relevant question to consider when it comes to finding the deeper meaning of forgiveness. Why? Because forgiveness isn't really for the wrongdoer. It's for whomever holds the grievance. I frequently hear my clients say, "Why should I be the one to forgive?" (Note the sore tone.)

The answer is simple: because you're the one hurting. Or smoldering. Or obsessing. Or ruminating. Or holding on. Or stuck in resentment. Our bitterness and resentment, even if understandable, binds us to the person who has hurt us. Perhaps we still love the person who has injured us. We may prefer to stay connected to them in a negative way rather than mentally sever ties. Holding on may be a protective measure to maintain our loyalty to someone or to keep from feeling alone. In many cases, the person who has wounded or betrayed us has now become a rationalization for not living our fullest life, our excuse for staying stuck.

By not letting someone go, we can cling to the hope that he or she is going to come back to us or admit their wrongdoing. Death, as mentioned, is not a foolproof way around this. I have seen many of my clients freeze their hearts in place while waiting for a deceased loved one to make things right, from the grave, before they can move forward. For anyone stuck here, the wait is interminable. Nothing, no goal or dream or ambition, is as important or compelling as the prospect of getting an apology from someone who has hurt us deeply. For when they do, in their hopeful imagination, the offending person will see their mistakes, understand the pain they have caused, say they are sorry, and render all things well. Shelved dreams can finally come to pass.

When stuck in resentment, we live in a suspended state of brooding. If intent on beating ourselves up, we can easily use our resentment as a weapon meant for the other person, but one which invariably snaps back to self-defeat. Indeed, there are many reasons why we hold onto our resentments. These are only a few. Regardless of the reason however, if we want to get unstuck and move on to a happier existence, we must forgive. Where do we begin when there seems to be so much riding on staying exactly where we are?

First, there are a few simple guidelines to follow, then some questions that can help to steer away from your own resistance.

## The Guidelines

1. Give yourself permission to get in touch, be present to, and tolerate all the feelings you are carrying, a little at a time.

2. Get out of your head (where you rationalize and "explain" your pain away) and move into the tender heart of your young self, the keeper of your true story. Your head is where you have made the messiness of your life neat and tidy by shoving it into the closet and then closed the

door on your vulnerability as a way of keeping yourself safe. There can be no real forgiveness without first allowing yourself to feel what you have buried inside. This is what it means to let yourself become vulnerable. By giving yourself access to your deepest emotions, the very ones you have cut yourself off from, you remove bricks from the psychological wall that has kept you closed in and others at a distance.

3. Let go of the rope.

Your willingness to feel your feelings, rather than remain in a mental tug-of-war with whomever has hurt, cheated, betrayed, left, or stole from you is the crucial step in ending the internal power struggle that has kept you tied to the offending person(s). Trying not to feel the anger, resentment, rage, and disappointment that you secretly hold toward others only ensures that you will lug it around longer. When you set the rope down and surrender to the facts as they are, you instantly move beyond the pseudo safety of stubbornness and righteousness and gravitate toward the truth and reality of your own history. It is only by acknowledging this reality that we come to have mastery over it. You will see that this is a vastly different experience than shrinking from the facts, running from them, or endlessly covering them up.

4. Don't romanticize, spiritualize, or intellectualize your feelings.

   Converting your feelings into Hallmarky or prosaic expressions will only help for the moment. Even deeply held spiritual beliefs, when relied upon in the service of *not* feeling, will not help to heal the wounds from your past. Truly restorative inner work occurs only when we admit, with equal parts brain and body, the realities of our past. Only when we can accept that the past happened exactly as it did can we actively and meaningfully minister to our own pain as the compassionate, emotionally competent, and insightful adult we have been waiting for our entire lives.

5. Don't worry.

   Forgiveness is not about condoning, excusing, or tolerating someone's bad behavior. It does not ask us to continue to be treated poorly or inappropriately. It will not turn you or me into doormats, wimps, or underlings. Quite the opposite; forgiveness allows us to assume a more grown-up stance in relationships, stepping out of the role of victim and into our whole, integrated selves. We interact more from a position of authority over ourselves, looking neither to dominate others nor be dominated. Forgiveness lessens the emotional inflammation that results from suppression of our true feelings and allows us to be on equal footing with everyone else. Quite a refreshingly radical way to live if you are used to feeling like a child in a room full of adults. We avoid the pitfalls and repetitive patterns that have contributed to our mistakes. We not only clean up our messes more quickly, we make fewer of them to begin with.

Forgiveness has a certain ring to it. It is the ring of clarity and presence over hiding and obfuscation. It brings with it the energetic flow that says, "I respect the reality of the situation," rather than the energetic drag associated with a refusal to accept what is. Does this mean we passively concede to pressure or circumstances? Do we resign ourselves to a way of thinking that suggests nothing can change or improve? Do we go through life without trying to effect change or growth? Do we yield to external circumstances as if in a hypnotic state? Absolutely not.

When we forgive others, that is to say let go of resentments, bitterness, regrets, living in the past *and* forgive ourselves, that is to say let go of self-blame, self-loathing, and living in a dulled state, something miraculous happens: we become empowered and we empower others. We harness the life force that was breathed into us and aim it at making the world and those of us who inhabit it a little better. The past is finally ushered to its rightful place: the past. Not right below the surface where its unresolved properties are easily triggered, and not tamped

so deep within that we are unaware of how it
runs us. Forgiveness invites us, indeed challenges us, to be who we have known ourselves to
be all along.

When my clients are struggling to find a forgiving path
through their deep pain, I ask them to consider the following questions. They've proved to be eye-opening as well as
heart-opening; and when answered in the context of the
guidelines you have just read; they can open doors you may
not have noticed before.

**A.** (I'll be honest. No one likes this one.) If the hurtful event
occurred in my adult years, did I contribute, knowingly or
otherwise, to the painful outcome?

Oftentimes, our blind spots prevent us from realizing
our contribution to strife, however small that contribution
may be. Blind spots in our personality include but are not
limited to: a defensive attitude, inability to tolerate uncertainty, an excessive need for validation from others, the need
to be right, rigidity, underlying unacknowledged anger, hy-
persensitivity to criticism, emotional emptiness, clinginess,
invulnerability, taking too many things personally, deflecting responsibility, and fear of conflict. There are others. The
point is, we readily see other peoples' flaws, limitations,
off-putting characteristics, annoying mannerisms, and weak-
nesses but are sometimes slow to see our own. Blind spots.
So called because they are outside our awareness. As a result,
we can be oblivious to our participation in an interpersonal
dynamic that goes south. Taking ourselves out of the victim
role (a role which makes forgiveness even more difficult) is

essential to unpacking a sticky or contentious situation. Recognizing that we may have had a hand in the problem, while perhaps hard to swallow, can make it easier to forgive.

We can turn our attention to the only thing we can control: our own behavior.

**B.** What can be learned from this experience? (No one likes this one very much, either.)

Nearly all experiences provide an opportunity for growth. By growth, I am referring to the skills one is called to develop to deal with a painful situation more effectively. If you feel you have been abandoned by someone for example, perhaps under the excruciating hurt that you are feeling is the chance to examine just how committed the other person really was. Were there some red flags that you detected but clearly overlooked because you did not want to be alone? In another instance, did your partner tell you repeatedly that your behavior (drinking, shopping, procrastinating, etc.) was a problem but you chose to tune that feedback out? If so, there is a chance that the pain of the situation is forcing you to look at your own denial. Situations and the lessons they pose often ask that we stretch ourselves to let something old out, or let something new in. Regardless of which it is, our capacity to reevaluate our beliefs and patterns is always being tested.

**C.** How might I use what I have learned from the experience to promote my own healing and support the healing of others?

There is something to be said for having been to hell and back while gaining a deeper understanding of your inner workings. You not only emerge more confidently, surer of your strengths, and better able to steer your own course, you naturally invite others to do the same. By adopting an attitude whereby you utilize your pain instead of futilely wishing it away, you experience a richer emotional life. Both the joyful love and poignant loss of an unfolding life become woven into the fabric of your being. You grow into a human being with greater depth and breadth, with an expanded capacity to appreciate the complexities of life.

## Perfectly Good Enough

Each of us is imperfect. Each of us has flaws. Each of us is worried about being judged by someone in some way if our failings and shame were to leak through our highly polished, hermetic facades. To other people, you and I are the ones who pose the threat. We are the ones whose judgments they are afraid of. Think about that: to everyone else, you and I are the "other person."

While we are so busy covering up our shadow selves because we fear judgment from the rest of the world, the rest of the world is hiding its shadow from us. You and I can either give our fellow humans good reason to worry about us, adding to layers of superficiality and subtle condemnation as we contribute to a collective anxiety, or we can bring a healing balm, a bit of sober acceptance to the world. By acknowledging the stupid, foolish, self-defeating, hurtful, dumb things we have done in our lives—with compassionate recognition—we stand a better chance of infusing the world with a little of the runoff. Until we make living safer for ourselves, we cannot make it safer for others.

Getting unstuck from our fears and stifling beliefs is about engaging in our lives from a place of enoughness. It is about embracing a perspective that says our legitimacy as a worthwhile person is not based on how glistening or squeaky clean our image is. Or how impeccably we present ourselves to the world. It is about knowing that our validity as well as our loving nature was established the moment we got here, whether we saw it reflected in the eyes of those who raised us. Though our elders and society tried (and very much succeeded) to get us to believe we had to earn it, just as they had been led to believe, the truth of the matter is you were enough the whole time. You are enough. You were enough. You have always been enough. Even when they couldn't see it.

If you feel a wave of resistance rise within you as these words reverberate in your head, and you are thinking you can't possibly claim this much positive self-regard in one gulp, relax.

Your enoughness does not make you special.

In fact, there are a few things about it that make you quite ordinary. First, your enoughness does not outshine anyone else's. It is no more and no less spectacular than that of any other person and as such, it cannot be quantified. Ultimately, you do not have anything in the worthiness department that every other human being doesn't also have. Their validity as a person and their right to be loved was also established the moment they got here, whether they are conscious of it or not. The worthiness playing field is not only level, it is endless. It is the wellspring of boundless possibility for us all. It is not earned, so it cannot be forfeited. It is not given so it cannot be taken away. It is something neither to feel prideful of nor uncomfortable about. It is one of the givens of life, like the inevitability of uncertainty, having two eyes, and knowing that things do not always go as planned. Your enough does not diminish anyone or anything. Quite the contrary. It elevates whomever and whatever it touches by inspiring others to engage up.

~

If the ideas in this book have prompted you in the slightest way to consider that beneath your striving, your comparing and despairing, and your stuckness, you are perfectly good enough exactly as you are, and always have been, I offer a word of caution: expect to be mildly to hugely uncomfortable as this realization hits. Why? Because you have been unfairly wrong about yourself for almost as long as you've been alive. You have been alternately racing then crawling on your belly then racing then crawling on your belly then racing westward, searching for your sunrise. You have been trying to prove what cannot be proved for it is beyond measure. You are weary from the effort. Feel your regret or grief or anger about your misdirection, but do not let it stop you from what is beginning to dawn. Recognize your bravery. Such a journey of introspection requires true courage. Anyone who reads this book is brave enough to step outside their comfort zone, beyond the story we tell ourselves that can be self-limiting.

An exploration into our deepest self is a process that requires that we no longer trivialize the ways in which we harm, cheat, or undermine ourselves, and by extension, others. By facing the consequences of deserting our authentic self, we can finally create the inner fortitude to have our own back, intelligently and responsibly. With *compassionate recognition*, we can begin to bridge the divide between our real self and our false self. We can remove blind spots. And as we do, obscured vision is replaced with greater clarity, and clarity is what we need to become unstuck and see a way forward.

I have seen hundreds of people get derailed in their lives, not because they made simple mistakes or even serious ones, but because they were too afraid to be themselves. By going to great lengths to perpetuate a myth of who they really are has driven many into walls of self-sabotage, blindness, and failure. Until we look inward to unpack and question the falsehoods we operate under, we run the risk of living according to the expectations of others. These expectations permeate our identity and we take them on as if they have always belonged to us. We lose sight of our true nature, true needs, and true feelings.

If we can lean toward them, where they can be understood, processed, and released, we have the best hope for a life in which we can thrive, whole and integrated, instead of merely surviving from one day to the next. Nothing short of this descent into the depths of our consciousness will allow us to confront our fears and provide the necessary and proper release of energy that has collected around them. This is what will ensure long-lasting peace of mind. Nothing feels as freeing as the knowledge that we are equipped to handle ourselves, that we no longer must live like fugitives on a desperate and never-ending escape from ourselves. Let me reassure you, self-honesty outweighs self-deceit. The way to grow more comfortable in your own skin is by choosing to be realistic with yourself, about yourself.

The violet and gold sunrise of your life is upon you. Go east.

# Suggested Reading and Resources

*Bird by Bird: Some Instructions on Writing and Life* by Anne Lamott, Anchor, September 1, 1995

*Honoring the Self: Self-Esteem and Personal Transformation* by Nathaniel Branden, Bantam Books, 1983

*The Body Keeps the Score: Brain, Mind and Body in the Healing of Trauma* by Bessel van der Kolk, Penguin Books, 2014

*The Disowned Self: An Illuminating Analysis of One of the Most Important Problems of Our Time: Self-Alienation* by Nathaniel Branden, Bantam Books, 1971

*The Genie in Your Genes: Epigenetic Medicine and the New Biology of Intention* by Dawson Church, Energy Psychology Press, May 15, 2014

*The New York Times*, "A Revolutionary Approach to Treating PTSD," May, 2014. www.nytimes.com/2014/05/25/magazine/a-revolutionary-approach-to-treating-ptsd.html

*The New York Times*, "How to Rewire Your Traumatized Brain," October, 2018. www.nytimes.com/2018/10/18/books/review/how-to-rewire-your-traumatized-brain.html

*The Science Behind Tapping: A Proven Stress Management Technique for the Mind and Body* by Peta Stapleton, Hay House Inc, April 16, 2019

*The Shadow Effect: Illuminating the Hidden Power of Your True Self* by Deepak Chopra, Debbie Ford, and Marianne Williamson, Harper One, 2010

*Think Like a Shrink: Solve Your Problems Yourself with Short-Term Therapy Techniques* by Christ Zois with Patricia Fogarty, Warner Books Inc, 1992

*Energy Healing: Simple and Effective Practices to Become Your Own Healer* by Kris Ferraro, St. Martin's Press, 2019

*How to be a Great Detective: The Hand-Dandy Guide to Using Kindness, Compassion and Curiosity to Resolve Emotional, Mental & Physical Upsets: For Tappers, Practitioners and Caregivers* by Jondi Whitis, CreateSpace, April 2017

## *For Further EFT Study:*

EFT International
www.eftinternational.org

EFT Universe
www.eftuniverse.com

*The Gold Standard EFT*, Tapping Training Materials and Tutorials by Gary Craig
www.emofree.com

# Acknowledgments

Although I wrote this book, in a very real sense it was co-authored by the clients I have known over the course of my career. Written in my words but expressed through their vulnerability, courage, and resilience, these pages reflect conversations and partnerships, each one special to me. I extend my appreciation to those I have worked with in therapy, at my self-esteem workshops, and VIP coaching weekends. Please accept my heartfelt gratitude. I hope you know that by doing so, you deepen it.

To the midwives, cheerers, and villagers:

To my discerning editor, for taking my manuscript and enthusiastically and insightfully turning it into a more coherent and readable version of itself, thank you, Marly Cornell.

To Ryan Scheife, the eye behind this book, your talent made typewritten words come to life. Thank you for your calm direction and expert guidance.

To Lisa Bobby, who accompanied me on my writing "retreats," and kept the fireplace, pinot noir, and talks about our respective shadows going, I am in debt of your patience and support.

To Puja Kanth Alfred, one of my most respected colleagues, it has become my good, good fortune to call you my friend. For your willingness to review the manuscript and grace it with your kind remarks, I am humbled and so very touched.

For those who have not only enhanced my EFT journey with their expertise but shaped it with their kindness and generosity, I thank my mentors:

To Jondi Whitis, I offer my heartfelt gratitude for your gentleness, creativity, availability, and laughter. If making someone feel safe is the first requisite of embracing one's shadow, you offered me an endless supply.

To Carol Look, were it not for mistakenly signing up for your live presentation in Stamford, Connecticut, in 2010, and witnessing your intuitive gift (I still call you "the client whisperer"), I may never have embarked on this career changing journey, I offer my sincerest admiration and gratefulness.

To Gary Craig who revolutionized self-help with the development of EFT tapping, many people are walking around emotionally freer because of you. I among them. Thank you, thank you.

To Linda Pashman, LCSW, you were a beacon during some choppy waters. Your depth of knowledge and openness of heart steadied me more than a few times. I will forget neither your warmth nor your honesty, ever.

To Michael Alpert, MD, you give psychiatry its good name and empathy its rightful place in psychotherapy. So much of what I learned about being a therapist I learned from you.

To Diana Fosha, PhD, before meeting you, I was not familiar with either hummus or unconditional support of my inner work. I now know that both are delicious and indispensable to my life.

To Heidi Garis, Tina Marian, Marti Murphy, Lynn Rekvig, Betty Steinman, and Leslie Vellios, my sister coaches and colleagues, the rawness that we shared during our training together and the healing afforded me by your willingness to see me at my most vulnerable, has helped me to recover a lost part of myself. Our connection will stay with me, always.

To Dee Anderson, writing coach and all-around good person to have in your corner, thank you for your consistent encouragement.

For digging me out of tech jams (there were many) and so much more, many thanks to my personal geek squad, Christie Schwaikert and Rachel Bogan. You two are simply the best.

For reading excerpts of this book and offering your feedback, critique, suggestions, and interest, I thank: Trish, Kim, Wendy, Irina, Becky, Mitzi, Nicole, Kyle, Miriam, Anita, Fabiola, Colleen, Diana, Diane, Michele, Mike, Mercy, Jen, Marcy, Rachel, Lauren, Linda, Vin, Michelle, Nicole, Helene, Deb, Jaime, Tamar, Leah, Loretta, Deni—villagers all.

For nudging me and brainstorming with me, often over her freshly baked Italian cookies, my warmest thanks to Kat Imbrogno.

And finally, to Dawn, my partner of almost thirty-nine years. We've been together this long because of your capacity and willingness to see and love me both masked and unmasked. For you, it seems to have made no difference at all which, in turn, has made all the difference in the world for me. You and Gabriella have all four chambers of my heart.

P.S. Thank you for telling me that my eyes aren't really that close together.

# Catherine Duca

*Author – Speaker – Trainer - Practitioner*

Catherine Duca is a Self-Esteem Expert, author, speaker, trainer, psychotherapist, and EFT (Emotional Freedom Techniques) practitioner. After becoming her own first EFT client, she began removing some of her stubborn emotional blocks herself. She then combined her extensive clinical background with these cutting-edge mindset tools and has taught hundreds of people worldwide over the last decade do the same.

Catherine's passion is helping her clients overcome their confidence blocks so they can become who they are truly meant to be. Her style has been described as one-part spin instructor, one-part empathic friend, one-part insightful teacher.

She earned a MSW at Rutgers University. She also trained at the Institute for Accelerated Empathic Therapy in NYC and was later invited to join the faculty as an adjunct instructor.

Catherine's career dates to her early twenties when she was the owner of Duca's Dogs, a hot dog truck. She sold hot dogs on a busy street corner in a New York metro suburb. Her many customers came for the frankfurter but often remarked that they left feeling listened to and understood. Through her speaking, training and books, her audiences and clients still leave feeling heard, nourished, and affirmed.

She maintains a private practice in New York City and Montclair, New Jersey, and lives with her partner, Dawn, and their morkie, Gabriella, in Montclair, New Jersey.

**Confidence Creation Blueprint** is Catherin's signature program. This customized, 2-day EFT tapping weekend is designed to help you unmask your blocks, harness the power of your true self, and master the confidence to say YES to the things that truly matter most to you.

~

**Learn More. Please Visit:**

*www.CatherineDuca.com*

CPSIA information can be obtained
at www.ICGtesting.com
Printed in the USA
LVHW021239260121
677513LV00004B/345